Praise for *Beyond Wiping Noses*

Beyond Wiping Noses is a book that is refreshingly readable and actionable but also evidence-based and rigorous. As Stephen says, the journey of becoming more informed – 'of moving away from mere practice towards deliberate, thoughtful praxis' – is an interesting and intelligent one.

Professor Samantha Twiselton, Director, Sheffield
Institute of Education, and Vice President
(external), The Chartered College of Teaching

Stephen Lane has rightly identified the paucity in research on the pastoral side of working with children in today's schools. In *Beyond Wiping Noses* he shepherds us through a wide-ranging tour of his thoughts on matters pastoral, challenging the long-held sense that it is best undertaken only by those with the instinct and feel for how best to support the welfare, wellbeing and emotional development of children. Colleagues in schools, and those entering the profession, will find this book a thought-provoking and stimulating read.

Jarlath O'Brien, author of *Better Behaviour: A Guide for Teachers*

An engaging and thought-provoking journey through the multifarious aspects of pastoral provision, offering readers a plethora of practical suggestions which may support classroom teachers to promote higher levels of school wellbeing.

Sarah Mullin, deputy head teacher
and author of *What They Didn't Teach Me on My PGCE*

Amongst the clamour and noise surrounding cognitive science, evidence-based practice and knowledge-rich curricula, little to no mention has been made of the pastoral dimension to education. Despite the slow emergence of the academic side of teaching into the light of research and evidence, pastoral work seems rooted in folk wisdom and gut instinct. This remarkable work by Stephen Lane bridges that gap, tying together these different worlds in a clear and well-researched book. Lane's breadth of reading is truly impressive, and he writes with authority on a range of thinkers and academics, distilling with ease ideas from Foucault, Biesta, Kirschner, Counsell and more.

Beyond Wiping Noses should be the starting point for everyone involved in pastoral work – and, accepting the argument that Lane makes from the outset, that means all of us.

Adam Boxer, Head of Science, The Totteridge Academy

Before reading *Beyond Wiping Noses* I was completely in the dark about the research available to help teachers inform their pastoral practices in school. This book helps to cut through the confusion and mixed messages over the kind of pastoral care that schools can and should offer, and places it into a wider context of curriculum and pedagogical thinking that teachers and school leaders may be more familiar with.

Beyond Wiping Noses needs to not only be read by pastoral leads but by all teachers and school leaders who play a role in helping the children in their care through the trials and tribulations of school life.

Mark Enser, Head of Geography and Research Lead, Heathfield Community College, *TES* columnist and author of *Teach Like Nobody's Watching*

Stephen Lane gives hope and strength to anyone who feels that schools can sometimes forget to relate to the whole child or leave some children behind in the drive for academic results. He approaches a fundamental but somewhat neglected area of school life, and shines a light on these vital issues with rigour, sensitivity and reference to evidence-based practice. In doing so he has created a bible for any teacher or school leader whose concern is the wellbeing of their pupils. A particular strength of the book is the way he marries a comprehensive overview of the theory with practical suggestions for day-to-day school life. I would urge all schools to have a copy of *Beyond Wiping Noses* in their staffroom.

Peter Nelmes, school leader and author of *Troubled Hearts, Troubled Minds: Making Sense of the Emotional Dimension of Learning*

Beyond Wiping Noses is a comprehensive exploration of what pastoral care is in schools. It also offers a detailed and balanced examination of how a pastoral curriculum could become an evidence-informed provision in schools, something which is often neglected in discussions around pastoral provision.

Too often, evidence focuses solely on teaching and learning and neglects the pastoral. This book very effectively bridges the two:

showing how research evidence can be applied in pastoral care, while also exploring a range of interesting sources of research that all pastoral leaders need to know about.

This is a must-read for anyone working in or aspiring to pastoral leadership. It is also important reading for anyone aspiring to senior leadership, where a balanced and nuanced understanding of pastoral provision is essential.

Amy Forrester, Director of Pastoral Care –
Key Stage 4, Cockermouth School

What is clear about this book by Stephen Lane is that there is an overdue need for all those involved in pastoral care and leadership to question what is right, what is needed and how to create schools that place humanity and the safeguarding of children and young people at their heart.

From behaviour management, bullying and restorative practice to computational thinking, cognitive load theory and much more, this book is jam-packed with gems of brilliance. A balanced critique of literature and educational approaches to ways of supporting children and young people is crucial, and this is Stephen's mission: getting us to reflect on what we offer and how we offer it, and suggesting ways to develop an even better pastoral care system in our school. His support of the four Cs – care, curriculum, cultivation and congregation – will resonate in my heart and mind for a considerable time.

Beyond Wiping Noses is a gem of a book. Read it and make use of it to question the pastoral care system in your own school and how you can ensure it meets everyone's needs.

Nina Jackson, education consultant, Teach Learn Create Ltd, author,
mental health adviser and award-winning motivational speaker

Beyond Wiping Noses is a much-needed and wonderfully refreshing, thought-provoking and uplifting read. Such a careful and intelligent explication of the theory, philosophy and policy that lie behind pastoral practice is an essential resource for any school leader, and indeed all staff, involved in pastoral work.

Lane weaves together strands from key thinkers such as Dewey, Biesta and Foucault to present a model of pragmatic pastoral praxis – providing substance to an often ill-defined area, giving shape to what research-informed pastoral work might look like, and offering an inspirational and deeply human call to 'extend beyond the utilitarian to develop a hopeful optimism'. In this unhiding of the pastoral curriculum, Lane challenges us to reflect on the nature of our assemblies, form time, everyday interactions with pupils, the curricular links between these elements, and the links with other subjects such as PSHE and SMSC.

The reflective, intentional and integrated approach manifested throughout *Beyond Wiping Noses* is an invaluable contribution to the education literature and will undoubtedly contribute to something of a revolution in the way pastoral work is thought about and enacted in our schools.

Ruth Ashbee, Assistant Head Teacher – Curriculum,
The Telford Priory School

Beyond Wiping Noses carefully navigates the paths through the pastoral life of a school leader and weaves theory with practical suggestions for a wide scope of issues – including bullying, behaviour systems, the pastoral curriculum and character education, as well as many other relevant and contemporary pastoral issues.

Stephen Lane explores the pertinence of educational research but acknowledges its limitations, especially when applied to truly human contexts. He is also insightful in his appreciation of contextual differences and the challenges that these may present. Although the text is often grounded in the debates and discussions seen on edu-Twitter, this need not alienate those who do not tweet, for the issues raised in *Beyond Wiping Noses* are pertinent and the Twitter debate is often reflected in 'real life' staffrooms nationally.

This book is detailed, thoughtful and very *human*; there's a sense of the person behind the writing, and an appreciation of the human behind the eyes of the reader.

Sarah Barker, English teacher, Orchard School Bristol,
writer and blogger

Stephen Lane
@sputniksteve

Beyond
Wiping
Noses

Building an informed approach to pastoral leadership in schools

Crown House Publishing Limited
www.crownhouse.co.uk

First published by

Crown House Publishing Limited
Crown Buildings, Bancyfelin, Carmarthen, Wales, SA33 5ND, UK
www.crownhouse.co.uk

and

Crown House Publishing Company LLC
PO Box 2223, Williston, VT 05495, USA
www.crownhousepublishing.com

First published 2020.

Cover image © dglimages – stock.adobe.com.

Crown House Publishing has no responsibility for the persistence
or accuracy of URLs for external or third-party websites referred to
in this publication, and does not guarantee that any content on
such websites is, or will remain, accurate or appropriate.

Quotes from Ofsted documents used in this publication have been
approved under an Open Government Licence. Please visit http://www.
nationalarchives.gov.uk/doc/open-government-licence/version/3/.

British Library Cataloguing-in-Publication Data

A catalogue entry for this book is available from the British Library.

Print ISBN 978-178583504-9
Mobi ISBN 978-178583512-4
ePub ISBN 978-178583513-1
ePDF ISBN 978-178583514-8

LCCN 2020941184

Printed and bound in the UK by
Gomer Press, Llandysul, Ceredigion

This book is dedicated to Mrs Sputnik.
No words can fully encapsulate why, but thank you.

And to my daughters. Because.

Acknowledgements

I wish to thank my Twitter buddies. All of the encouragement, support and friendship there has been phenomenal. Cut through all the nonsense of edu-Twitter and you can find some genuinely good folk.

Huge thanks to David and the team at Crown House Publishing, whose work is extraordinary. Particularly, eternal thanks to Louise for bearing with me and making these words carry some semblance of sense.

I would also like to say a big thank you to Claire Stoneman, who got me thinking about all of this.

Contents

Acknowledgements .... *i*

Foreword vii

Safeguarding ix

Introduction 1

Chapter 1: Pastoral Roles 7

    Introduction 7

    The Form Tutor 8

    Head of Year 10

    The School 'Chaplain' 15

    Head of Wellbeing 16

    School Counsellor 17

    Designated Senior Lead for Mental Health (DSLMH) 18

    Conclusion 19

Chapter 2: What Research? 21

    Introduction 21

    The Gold Standard 22

    Effect Sizes 23

    Being Critical 26

    Where Can I Find Pastoral Research? 34

    CLT and Rosenshine 36

    Conclusion 38

Chapter 3: A Knowledge-Rich Pastoral Curriculum 39

    Introduction 39

    PSHE Education, Citizenship and SMSC 40

    Relationships and Sex Education 46

The Hidden Curriculum 49

The Book of Common Prayer and the Golden Rule 51

Self-Knowledge 54

Conclusion 55

Chapter 4: Bullying 57

Introduction 57

Conflict and Relational Bullying 59

Systemic Bullying 62

Cyberbullying 64

Intervention Strategies 66

Conclusion 68

Chapter 5: Wellbeing, Mental Health and Attachment 71

Introduction 71

The Role of Schools 73

Sadfishing and Social Media 75

Direct Instruction, Project Follow Through, Self-Esteem
and Praise 78

Attachment Theory 81

Conclusion 83

Chapter 6: Behaviour 85

Introduction 85

Approaches to Behaviour Management 87

No Excuses for Zero Tolerance 88

No More Exclusions 92

Restorative Practice 93

Warmstrict 96

Practicalities 97

Conclusion 100

Chapter 7: Character 103
    Introduction 103
    Defining Character Education 105
    Doing Character Education 106
    Looking for Rubies 111
    Watch and Punish 112
    Conclusion 117

Chapter 8: Remote Pastoral 119
    Introduction 119
    Homeschooling 121
    Conclusion 122

Conclusion 125

References and Further Reading 127

About the Author 142

Foreword

I loved being a form tutor. I had the same group throughout their progression through the school from Year 7 to Year 11. As I was a newly qualified teacher (NQT) at the time, I felt I grew up professionally with them. They taught me a lot. I became aware quite early on, however, that while I'd had pretty good support both as an NQT and early career professional as far as my subject was concerned, the same did not hold true for my pastoral role. When I asked the senior leader who 'led on CPD' (and who discharged his responsibility for this aspect of his work by putting the odd flier about subject-specific courses in our pigeonholes) whether there were any courses on being a form tutor, he looked surprised and said that he didn't think there were as he hadn't come across any, before also commenting that it was probably a good idea. Nothing further was heard or done about it.

This was the early 1990s and there was no internet, certainly not in schools, so if it didn't land in your pigeonhole, your sources of information were pretty limited. Fortunately, there were good folk I could call on, compare notes with, and I generally bumbled through – but there was nothing systematic that I could draw on. A further indicator of the fact that this role was not taken seriously was that being a form tutor did not come up in any of the professional conversations and appraisal of my teaching work. It was as though it just 'happened'.

And it turns out that not a huge amount has changed in the decades since. At the end of a webinar with school colleagues yesterday afternoon, there was a question about further professional reading, including whether I could suggest any texts that could develop the role of pastoral leaders. Fortunately, I was able to recommend Stephen's book, but it has to be said that there is a dearth of literature on this important aspect of school provision. And it is for this reason that *Beyond Wiping Noses* is very welcome.

As Stephen notes, the status of the form tutor has not really been discussed for over twenty years, either formally or informally (on social media or otherwise). It is a shame that this role which has the potential to make a difference to young people has been neglected for so long. Ofsted's (2019b) *Education Inspection Framework* might help to open up conversations and more opportunities for tutors to reflect on this aspect of their work. In the personal development judgement it refers to the extent to which the curriculum and the provider's wider work support learners to develop their resilience, confidence and independence - fertile ground I would suggest for thinking about this in relation to the role of the form tutor.

Stephen provides some fascinating insights as he gets to the heart of what a pastoral role entails, and in considering the role through a range of different lenses - from the 'golden rule' to character education to cyberbullying - and offers us ways in which we might amplify this aspect of school provision. And, in doing so, he makes the case for building an informed approach to pastoral leadership in schools.

Having established that the pastoral role is a remarkably under-researched area of provision, Stephen considers some of the insights from cognitive science and learning research which might throw light on pastoral work. These are particularly fruitful, and it is good to see that decades-old wisdom - for example, from Michael Marland's (1974) classic work *Pastoral Care* - is referenced in this book. And it is Marland who was one of the founders of the National Association for Pastoral Care in Education (NAPCE).

Each chapter concludes with some top tips to help embed this work - for example, the exemplary advice from Bill Rogers and others in encouraging teachers and form tutors to think in advance about their responses to challenging behaviour and to prepare a 'script' which could be used to frame these difficult conversations.

Ultimately, *Beyond Wiping Noses* will take us some way towards opening up discussions about what a pastoral role might entail. This is important because for much of the sector it is a 'hidden' curriculum of social practices and expectations - and in becoming more deliberate about our work in this area, we will enhance the status of this aspect of pupils' experience in school.

Mary Myatt

Safeguarding

Before we begin, a note on safeguarding. If you have not received any recent safeguarding training in your school, go speak to your designated safeguarding lead (DSL) right now. If you don't know who your DSL is, go speak to your head teacher right now.

Safeguarding policy is the single most important thing that all those working with children and young people need to know. If you are working in schools in any capacity then you are required to at least be familiar with the publication *Keeping Children Safe in Education* (Department for Education, 2019c).

It is not within the intended scope of this book to discuss the topic of safeguarding any further than to insist that you ensure your safeguarding training is up to date and that you have read the key documents. If you are a school leader, you must ensure that your staff - all of them - have read these documents and received the required training. If you are reading this book in school right now, stop. Email a copy of *Keeping Children Safe in Education* to all your staff with a read receipt request. Get your HR person to check the records to ensure that everyone on staff has received the required training. If you are reading this after hours, have safeguarding as your first action point for tomorrow. Put safeguarding on every meeting agenda. Put safeguarding at the heart of every conversation.

Introduction

I have been a keen advocate of research- and evidence-informed practice in teaching for a number of years. I have established a reputation with colleagues as quite well-versed – authoritative, even – on the subject. After all, I have attended and spoken at conferences, offering my plus-one tickets to colleagues; I have shared research papers with colleagues and delivered INSET on topics such as cognitive load theory (CLT); I have adapted my classroom teaching to include retrieval practice, dual coding and interleaving; I have argued on Twitter over what constitutes 'research' and whether teachers could ever truly be 'researchers'; I have mentored trainee teachers and discussed with them the power of the testing effect; I've written training materials about how to apply Rosenshine's (2012) principles of instruction in the English classroom. But when I was asked to deliver a session at researchEDBrum on how I use research and evidence in my pastoral role, I was hit by an unnerving realisation: I don't.

The truth is that teaching is generally not (yet) a research- or evidence-informed profession. The frequently trotted out analogy of medicine, whilst problematic, at least gives some interesting points of contrast. Nurses, for example, are required to demonstrate a commitment to relevant ongoing training in order to maintain their registration.

A key word search for the term 'research' conducted on the teaching vacancies section of the *TES* website, compared with the equivalents for the *BMJ* and *Nursing Times*, is pretty revealing. On 4 September 2019 – the day I happened to be looking into this – there were 'over 2,833' jobs advertised on the *TES* website.[1] Of these, four contained the key word 'research'. However, three were from the same school, which happens to have the word 'research' in its name. The remaining position was for a 'database and

---

1   See https://www.tes.com/jobs. Data gathered 4 September 2019. *TES* total number of jobs advertised was 2,833; number of jobs containing the term 'research' was 1: 0.04%. *BMJ* total number of jobs advertised was 575; number of jobs containing the term 'research' was 167: 29.04%. *Nursing Times* total number of jobs advertised was 155; number of jobs containing the term 'research' was 26: 16.77%.

research manager' role, designed to support fundraising activities. So, one job in 2,833 – that's 0.04% – uses the word 'research', but this is not directly related to any aspect of the actual work of teaching – academic or otherwise.

By comparison, both the *BMJ*[2] and *Nursing Times*[3] websites advertised far more job listings featuring the word 'research': 29% and 17% respectively. Whilst a small number of these may be due to the term being part of a hospital name, for example, the vast majority do in fact refer to research in the job outlines. For instance, one vacancy on the *Nursing Times* website says: 'You'll demonstrate good clinical practice at all times and be accountable for own actions and contribute to the setting of clinical standards, policy and procedures and research based care and other practice development initiatives.' I've yet to see any job advertised on the *TES* that includes a specific commitment to research-based practice.

Goldacre (2013, p. 7) has been a vocal proponent of research-informed practice in education, seeing it as a 'huge prize waiting to be claimed by teachers', but it seems that his call for education to follow in the footsteps of medicine has not yet been heeded across the field. Thankfully, there is clearly a growing interest in, and support for, research-informed practice in teaching, as evidenced by the huge success of researchED, the rise of Research Schools, and access to research journals through the Chartered College of Teaching and its in-house journal *Impact*. The Department for Education has thrown its weight behind research-informed practice too, with Nick Gibb speaking at a number of researchED conferences to highlight its importance (e.g. Department for Education and Gibb, 2015, 2018).

However, much of the discourse around research-informed practice in education is about domain-specific pedagogy – that is, teaching subject knowledge – and is increasingly dominated by CLT, retrieval practice and the definition of learning as adding to long-term memory (Clark et al., 2012). Whilst this domain-specific pedagogical application of research is clearly important, it seems to me that an

---

2 See https://jobs.bmj.com.
3 See https://www.nursingtimesjobs.com.

essential aspect of teaching is potentially being neglected – the pastoral aspect. If pedagogy is still lagging in terms of the application of research to practice, then the pastoral aspect of teaching is woefully poorly served. In my experience – having worked in many different schools over two decades – pastoral work is often ad hoc and reactive. Many schools have systems and routines in place, such as tariffs of sanctions for misbehaviour, but none in my experience have adopted a research- or evidence-informed approach to the pastoral. With the exception of safeguarding, there is no body of literature to which teachers can make reference in their discussions, no procedures which rely on case studies, and no equivalent of the British National Formulary, whose publications 'reflect current best practice as well as legal and professional guidelines relating to the uses of medicines'.[4] There is no equivalent of the National Institute for Health and Care Excellence (NICE), the medical regulatory body which publishes industry guidelines, to supervise interventions. And yet the ways in which teachers respond to pastoral issues can have long-lasting consequences for the children in their care, and the lack of consistency between – and even within – schools is potentially problematic.

The problem also works the other way around: trying to find relevant literature by searching on an online book retailer's website for the key term 'head of year' yields very few results, and doing a literature search through my university's library portal yields only a few items of relevance. The term 'pastoral leader' returns just as little. All of which suggests that the notion of being a research- and/or evidence-informed pastoral practitioner is still entirely novel.

This is worrying and yet unsurprising. In Chapter 1, I will explore how many teachers regard the pastoral as less important than the academic: they don't like being form tutors, and they find the pastoral hard. And yet, with the increased focus on mental health and wellbeing, along with the increase in concerns over cyberbullying and the negative effects of social media use, the pastoral is arguably more important than ever. Schools, at least, do acknowledge the importance of the pastoral: it is common to find responsibility

---

4   See https://www.bnf.org/about/.

for it designated to a member of the senior leadership team (SLT), along with other common pastoral roles such as heads of year, heads of house and, of course, form tutors. But, whilst the educational discourse is alive with discussions about research-informed approaches to classroom pedagogy, alongside the recent prominence of curriculum, the pastoral is seriously under-represented.

My journey in teaching began back in 1998, when I embarked on a BEd in secondary English at Newman College of Higher Education in Birmingham (now Newman University). I loved it. I enjoyed the subject specialism aspects of the course – literature, linguistics and a bit of drama too. I loved the pedagogy aspects of it: discussing approaches to teaching and learning, and the modules on professional studies – just being involved in that discourse was exciting, challenging and stimulating. But I distinctly remember being particularly fond of the pastoral aspects of the course, especially the modules on the social, moral, spiritual and cultural (SMSC) elements of schooling. The pastoral aspects were a significant feature of my initial teacher training (ITT), but over the decades I have worked in schools that are increasingly subjected to accountability measures which have moved the language of meetings and 'training', and the daily discussions of the staffroom, away from the pastoral needs of students and towards the requirements of statistical analysis and the inspectorate. Performance management has been centred upon percentages of students attaining target grades, themselves based upon dubious statistical claims. Teachers have been judged using Ofsted grades, based on observations of the unobservable. School leaders now speak of 'buckets' and Progress 8 scores (see Ing, 2018).

Moving into the independent sector was startling. I was taken back to the cruciality of the pastoral, with students seen as 'glorious individuals' (to quote my current head teacher). Of course, there are many schools where this might be the case. Since joining Twitter and engaging with the network of educators that it enables, I have been reassured to see many school leaders proclaiming their visions for schooling, pedagogy and the curriculum with the aim of empowering students to engage in the great conversations of humanity (Arnold, 1869). It has been invigorating to see the rise of the researchED community and the Chartered College of Teaching championing the power of research-informed approaches. I have been an ardent supporter of the research movement.

I am now a regular at researchED events and am a founding fellow of the Chartered College of Teaching. I have adapted my own teaching practice, and shout from the rooftops about Rosenshine and CLT. So it was with a dawning sense of humbling embarrassment that I realised, when I was asked to give a talk on how I use research in my pastoral role, that my work as head of year was frequently reactive and instinctive, and that I had not read a single paper on pastoral care since I completed my BEd in 2001. I set about addressing that, and discovered – amongst other things – a set of resources through the journal *Pastoral Care in Education*. Immediately, I began to see ways to improve my practice in relation to a particular pastoral issue and, by extension, to improve the experience of the students in my care.

This book is a reflection of the journey I have taken towards a more informed response to pastoral matters. Although my route takes in some scholarly scenery, this is not an academic treatise. It has not been peer-reviewed, and I do not claim to have conducted rigorous or thorough literature reviews. There are no claims to definitive answers here, but the book serves to support the reader in building their own research-informed approach to pastoral leadership. Each chapter points to some key themes, ideas and sources, before offering suggestions for changes to practice.

Chapter 1

Pastoral Roles

Introduction

All teachers are pastoral leaders. This may not be welcome news for some of them though. Judging by a Twitter poll I ran in December 2019, over a third of teachers do not like being a form tutor: many of the comments I received in reply articulated negative feelings.[1] Some respondents find the pastoral hard, and some demonstrated a clear distinction between the academic and the pastoral, suggesting that the latter should be left for those with a 'passion' for it. I think this reflects a worrying tendency in many schools for the pastoral to be treated as a bolt-on to what is seen as their main work - academic attainment, especially in the secondary sector (where I am based). Here, teachers are subject specialists, having most likely completed a subject-based degree before a one-year teacher training course. Some of these courses include strong pastoral elements, but many do not. Many ITT providers are based in schools where pastoral provision might be patchy at best.

Every teacher - indeed, every adult in the school - has a pastoral duty: an obligation to put safeguarding at the forefront of their work and to be mindful of the students' wellbeing. In a conversation about this on Twitter, one contributor pointed out the vital role played by her daughter's school librarian in doing more to keep her daughter 'happy, safe & able to attend school than any other member of staff'.[2] However, there are roles within the school designed specifically to focus on pastoral care.

---

1 Twitter poll, 17 December 2019. Available at: https://twitter.com/sputniksteve/status/1206990556590673920?s=20.

2 See https://twitter.com/eleonorasfalcon/status/1213431798014853121?s=20.

The Form Tutor

Not all teachers are form tutors. Often, those with managerial posts, such as heads of department, are 'relieved' of the requirement to be form tutors in order to give them additional management time. In my current role as head of year, I do not have a form. This enables me to visit other teachers' forms in the morning and affords me time to deal with any pastoral issues that may have arisen. Sometimes, part-time teachers might not have a form. There may be a whole variety of other reasons why teachers might not be form tutors.

The form tutor role usually involves greeting the students at the start of the day for formal registration in 'form time', during which administrative tasks are often carried out – checking planners, checking uniform, conveying messages and so on. But its importance goes beyond the administrative. For some, form time represents the buffer zone between *out there* and *in here*, where *in here* is the school day. Form time is the transition time between *not school* and *in school and learning*. Some tutors like to cultivate an informal space, or perhaps a semi-formal space, where the transition occurs during the ten or fifteen minutes available. For others, the transition occurs at the threshold of the form room: as students enter, they are expected to immediately transition into 'school mode', adopting the appropriate mental stance, ensuring their uniform is correct before coming in and so on. In some schools, form time is expected to be busy, with some personal, social, health, and economic (PSHE) education activities, a topical discussion or similar. In other cases, form time is for social cohesion: a time when students can chat, and the tutor joins in.

Students are often encouraged to cultivate a sense of ownership of the form room, perhaps by creating a wall display. The form tutor adopts the role of a nurturing guide – some more formal than others. Furthermore, the form tutor is often positioned as the first port of call if a student has any issues or questions, and the first port of call for parents too. In some schools the form tutor is more heavily involved in the students' daily affairs, but the role is fairly universally understood.

It is actually a fairly difficult role to balance. As a form tutor, the relationship you have with your students is not quite the same as it is if you teach those same students in your subject lessons. Judging the degree of formality can be tricky. Fostering a supportive, relaxed and warm atmosphere in form time, one which is also conducive to establishing a sense of preparedness for learning, can be as contradictory as trying to perform Hamlet's 'To be or not to be' soliloquy as a comedic mime. My solution as a form tutor was essentially to treat form time as a lesson, albeit a slightly more relaxed one.

Beyond the constraints of form time, though, the form tutor is, or at least should be, the first point of contact for pastoral issues that arise during the day. This can be very challenging, especially on days when you have a full teaching timetable, break duties and lunchtime meetings. Firstly, when do you find time to listen to your tutee's concerns? Secondly, when do you find time to pursue any follow-up, let alone complete any necessary paperwork? And what if the concern is a safeguarding one? What if, at the end of break-time when you've just come out of a staff briefing, you find little Gertrude is waiting outside the staffroom to tell you that she wants to die? But you've got double Year 11 next, and they're just three months away from their exams and the head teacher has made it very clear that Year 11 lessons must not be cancelled or missed or delayed and your performance management targets demand that 90% of them get grade 7 or above and they're the bottom set and if you're late they're going to be causing mayhem in the corridors and …

The pressure on teachers just to attend to their classes is immense; additional issues which can arise unexpectedly and have the potential to wipe out a day's teaching add fuel to an already precarious mix of volatile emotions. Hopefully, in most schools there is a good network of pastoral support structures: perhaps there are non-teaching pastoral support workers who can help a child in trauma; perhaps the head of year has a sensible timetable enabling them to support the child; perhaps there is a member of SLT who can assist. At the very least, you may have a sympathetic departmental colleague who could cover your Year 11 class for a while.

But, ultimately, the form tutor role is inevitably a bolt-on to being a 'teacher'. In job descriptions, pastoral aspects of the job are always included as core elements, but they are almost always listed after the academic elements. The status of the form tutor has not really been promoted in the literature either. Very little has been written specifically about the role since the 1990s or early 2000s and, like the pastoral in general, it has not been a significant feature in discussion on edu-Twitter or in the wider discourse of research-informed education practice. The more I think about it, the sadder I feel about this apparent neglect of the form tutor role, especially given its clear potential to have a positive impact on children and young people.

Head of Year

I love being a head of year, fraught though it is with the emotional carnage of childhood or – in my Key Stage 3 context – that vicious twilight zone of the emergent teenager. It's difficult to list all the things that we actually do in pastoral leadership roles – to precisely articulate the nuance of the situations that might arise, to catalogue the multitudinous decisions that we have to make on a daily basis, to fully chart the navigation of tempestuous social relationships, to index the infinite complexities of the endless variations in social, emotional and mental wellbeing that our students experience. And then there is the school context. Whilst there are, no doubt, a hundred commonalities across diverse school communities, there are surely thousands of context-dependent needs and demands that form tutors, heads of year and pastoral leaders must try to understand and negotiate in order to best serve those in our care.

Nevertheless, there is obviously a need to define the role of head of year (or pastoral leader), if only in order that such posts can be advertised and qualified in job descriptions. So, how would you do it? If you were going to write the job description for a head of year role, what would you include? What would be the first bullet point on the list? What would you prioritise? And, perhaps more interestingly, what would you omit?

Perusing the job adverts and accompanying descriptions on the *TES* website is, again, revealing. Many reflect a desire to find someone who can 'motivate' people; who shows 'enthusiasm, sensitivity, resilience and strong interpersonal skills'; someone who is 'inspirational'. Of course, they must be 'an outstanding and talented practitioner' because everyone must be 'outstanding' – it's a word which has probably done more harm to the teaching profession than any other. And this is the problem with this kind of language – or jargon – as it appears in so many of these advertisements: it's a sloganised managerialism full of clichés so cold they've been rendered ultimately meaningless. Do a search for the term 'passion' in teaching job adverts and behold the banality. This kind of wording says nothing about the job. Sure, it presents a kind of idealised set of aims, including the desire to improve 'young people's life chances', but there's nothing much there in terms of specifics. Meanwhile, job descriptions often include a lot of 'coordination', ensuring 'student progress' and reviewing attendance data. Whilst these tasks are perfectly reasonable and important, it strikes me that they are somewhat ... administrative, managerial, dry. There's also nothing there about commitment to professional growth or learning, and nothing at all about developing research- or evidence-informed policy or practice.

It could be argued that such job descriptions perpetuate what Lodge (2008, p. 5) sees as the persistence of 'dysfunctional interpretations' of the role of head of year: 'using the system for administration, as a watered-down welfare service, or for behaviour management'. Lodge goes on to present a phrase used by a group of head teachers with whom she was working which she claims 'poignantly captures two of these distortions: "wiping noses and kicking butts"' (p. 5). Lodge articulates frustration at the notion of the head of year role being about behaviour management – kicking butts – and we will take a look at this particular aspect of pastoral care in a later chapter. The notion that perhaps we ought to be moving beyond a view of the pastoral as 'wiping noses and kicking butts' is one that I can support.

Despite the vastness of the tangled web of all that the pastoral encompasses, it is nonetheless valuable to draw out some of these strands in an attempt to define what a pastoral leadership role might encompass. I'd recommend that you periodically write a list of what your role entails; this is a useful grounding exercise that can help to refocus your priorities in the most hectic of periods, and it could help to identify any areas where you might legitimately ask for support or delegate to others, such as form tutors. Better still, producing such a list in conjunction with colleagues might help to foster a collegial approach to pastoral work that would likely benefit the team and, most importantly, the children in your care. My list looks something like this:

- Safeguarding.
- Academic performance.
- Behaviour.
- Wellbeing.
- PSHE education.
- Assemblies.
- Counselling.
- Mentoring.
- Safeguarding.

You may think you've spotted an error there - the repetition of 'safeguarding'. I have spent some time mithering over whether that should be the first thing on my list or the last, and have decided that it should probably be both. Everyone who works with children should have safeguarding as their first and last thought.

But even a list like this doesn't adequately define the role of head of year. Helpfully, the National Association for Pastoral Care in Education (NAPCE) has composed its own guidance for pastoral support in schools, which inevitably takes the form of a long list (Jones, 2019). NAPCE does a decent job of encapsulating the plethora of particulars involved. It also succeeds, I think, in traversing the potential false dichotomy between the pastoral and the academic. It should be fairly obvious to most teachers that there is a symbiotic relationship between the academic and the pastoral.

There is also a strong emphasis in the NAPCE guidelines on personal development. It's worth noting, of course, that Ofsted's (2019b) *Education Inspection Framework* includes very specific references to learners' personal development. Indeed, personal development is one of the four key areas against which inspectors will make judgements, including about the extent to which 'the curriculum and the provider's wider work support learners to develop their character – including their resilience, confidence and independence – and help them know how to keep physically and mentally healthy' (Ofsted, 2019b, p. 11). It is also reassuring to see that the NAPCE guidelines place strong emphasis on the 'skills, knowledge and understanding of staff', including the suggested requirement that staff 'Take responsibility for remaining fully informed about developments in pastoral care and in education that have an impact on the support of learners in school' (Jones, 2019).

The pastoral is a vast ocean of sometimes perilous waters, but having a set of guidelines such as those offered by NAPCE can help us to navigate the tempestuous seas. However, it is also useful to have a macro view, an overriding sense of the purpose of any pastoral role. Sobel (2019, loc. 305) tells us that 'Whether you are a middle leader, working as a head of year or head of key stage, or are a senior leader responsible for pastoral care across your school, the main focus of your role is to provide effective care for the welfare, wellbeing and overall success of the students in your school'. He later provides this rather neat key takeaway: 'The most important aspect of the pastoral leadership role is to enable students to participate. No matter what your job description says, this is your fundamental purpose and your key to success, and can only be achieved through understanding' (loc. 371). From this, we can draw out these two statements of pastoral purpose:

1   To provide effective care for the welfare, wellbeing and overall success of the students in your school.
2   To enable students to participate.

Again, like 'form tutor', the term 'head of year' yields little in searches of the academic literature. I think this probably reflects the varied nature of the role, but it is interesting to note that there hasn't been much work done to explore that nature – or the purpose and impact of this ubiquitous role. Every secondary school has heads of year, even allowing for variations in nomenclature, such as year team leader. Some schools use 'vertical' tutoring, with form groups made up of students from different year groups. This structure is intended to encourage social cohesion across age groups, enable older students to act as mentors and role models for younger students, and reduce workload for teachers when it comes to report cycles. Schools have reported that vertical tutoring has reduced instances of bullying, amongst other positive effects.[3] However, in my own experience, the system creates mini-cliques or enclaves within form groups – the Year 7 students all sit together and so on. And far from reducing workload, it meant that I had far more mental plates to spin with regard to the differing demands of the year groups, such as options for Year 9 and GCSE revision sessions for Year 11.

I would be interested to know how the role of pastoral leader plays out in schools with vertical tutoring where, perhaps, head of house becomes equivalent to head of year. In some schools, head of house is an SLT position, perhaps an assistant head teacher role. I can imagine this working relatively well in terms of pastoral leaders having a broad oversight of a range of students, but I wonder if it might produce a somewhat fragmented perspective. But in any case, what I say here about heads of year applies equally to heads of house in schools where that is a pastoral leadership role.

In my setting, year groups are relatively small, so the head of year role in fact covers more than one year group. We have a head of Years 5 and 6, a head of Years 7 to 9, a head of Years 10 and 11, and a head of sixth form. These are middle leadership roles, the nomenclature for which is 'operational leadership'. Whatever this role is called in your school, it is important to develop a clear idea about what pastoral leadership entails within your context. Once you have established this, then you can begin to think about how you might develop an informed approach to each of the aspects involved.

---

3 See, for example, http://www.lawrencesheriffschool.net/about-us/values-and-ethos/vertical-tutoring.

policies rather than resources. Meanwhile, a quick search online shows a number of books released in 2019, or due in 2020, that have identified the obvious gap in the market.

One source of information that is very useful for teachers and older students is Brook, whose website offers resources and advice around a range of topics.[7] It is presented in a friendly online interface that gives information in a format that is easy to read and navigate. Interestingly, in a blog post for the Terrence Higgins Trust, Brook's head of policy highlights the need for RSE to be 'recognised as a specialist subject' and stresses that until it is, funding should be 'made available to support external sexual health experts in school' (Hallgarten, 2020).

The same can be said of PSHE education topics in general, but when it comes to RSE the issue is clear. Firstly, there is a real danger of teachers communicating incorrect information around the topic of sex and relationships to young people, just at the time when they are likely to be most vulnerable to misconceptions, myths and rumours. If we are going to do this, we need to get it right. Secondly, as noted earlier in the chapter, there may well be issues around embarrassment which could affect the delivery of this information.

A further source of specific resources for RSE is the aforementioned PSHE Association.[8] Of course, you might need to be a member to gain access, but institutional membership is less than the price of a supply teacher for one day. School leaders need to make decisions about how best to deploy their finances in support of the various programmes, initiatives and expectations on which they need to deliver. Do you pay for membership of an association, pay external speakers to deliver the content, buy a library full of books and ask teachers to train themselves, or a combination thereof?

Of course, RSE is not an uncontested area. There have been high-profile protests - gaining much media attention - by parents against the teaching of RSE, leading to legal action to prevent

---

7   See https://www.brook.org.uk.
8   See https://www.pshe-association.org.uk/statutory-tools.

these kinds of demonstrations (Busby, 2019). For some parents, there is a very genuine concern about teaching what they see as views which oppose their own firmly held religious beliefs (Ferguson, 2019). And whilst from September 2020 parents will not have the right to withdraw their children from relationships education or health education in primary school - or RSE or health education in secondary school - the nature of these topics remains incredibly sensitive.

Concerns around RSE are not limited to parents who hold religious concerns. The journal *Educational Theory* presented a special issue on the ethics of sex education, the introduction of which noted, 'Perhaps no other part of the school curriculum generates as much controversy and on such a consistent basis as sex education' (Corngold, 2013, p. 439). The articles in this special issue explore various related matters, such as ethics, morals and the history of sex education (for example, Lamb, 2013; Hand, 2013). Whilst many teachers would seek practical suggestions and resources to help them deliver RSE, I concur with Corngold (2013, p. 441) that 'Given that many of the issues surrounding it are value-laden, multifaceted, and (as noted) highly contentious, the topic of sex education begs for careful philosophical analysis', and I would very much encourage colleagues to engage with these kinds of debates.

Finding time to incorporate PSHE education, citizenship, SMSC, RSE and any other aspect of what might be considered important is inevitably difficult. However, this is not in itself a sufficient argument against a pastoral curriculum; rather, it is evidence of the need to be selective about what might go into such a curriculum. School leaders must prioritise what should be taught, and how and when it should be taught. It is up to school leaders to determine how this pastoral knowledge should be assembled into a coherent sequence - conversations which I suspect do not happen enough.

The Hidden Curriculum

The notion of the hidden curriculum can be traced back to Jackson's *Life in Classrooms* (1968) and appears in work of the following decades which takes a critical (as in critical theory) approach. The hidden curriculum refers to the unwritten values, perspectives and beliefs that are transmitted in the classroom and around school. Critical work into the hidden curriculum finds that it maintains inequality by reinforcing gender stereotypes, capitalist social relations and the predominance of white institutions (Cotton et al., 2013).

The hidden curriculum is constructed of the messages that lie between the words. Children are required to navigate a complex web of unwritten rules about how the school operates as an institution (Jackson, 1968), but also how each individual teacher operates within each classroom – and this can change from one lesson to the next. But I am also conscious of the kinds of messages that run contrary to those which we might intend. For instance, what are the messages that we convey to children and young people in our assemblies?

In one school, each assembly (and there were two or three a week) was an opportunity for the head teacher to remind students in Year 11 that at least 70% of them were expected to gain a grade C or above in five or more subjects at GCSE (this was before the grading reforms in England). At the time, this was an aspirational target, and I imagine that the head teacher felt that he was being motivational with this spiel. But I couldn't help but feel for the students in the other 30% – students who no doubt knew that this expectation did not apply to them. How did this constant reminder affect them? What self-view might they have developed? What view did they hold of their position within the school community? What was their place? What was their value? What message were we giving to these students? In a cohort of 200, that is sixty kids. Sixty kids who, essentially, have been written off by the head teacher.

In a different school, in which I was tutor to a Year 10 form group, I recall an assembly which was intended to promote the notion of being extraordinary. This notion in itself is stupid, of course – how do we define the extraordinary? And can we expect all our students to accomplish the goal of becoming it? But I digress. The assembly involved the head of year showing a video which was a compilation of people doing 'extraordinary' things. Things like parkour. Things like standing on top of mountains. Things like riding a BMX bike down a ramp and over a ravine. Things like jumping onto moving cars. Yes. A Year 10 assembly in which students were encouraged to see a young man jumping onto a moving car as something to celebrate.

I suspect this assembly was the product of those old demons which curse us all: a lack of time to prepare properly – leading to a last-minute approach – and misguided good intentions. The wish to motivate students is perfectly understandable, but we need to think much more carefully about what we wish to motivate them about and towards. Motivation, of course, can be a strong driver of students' academic success and sense of self-worth (Hodis et al., 2011; Fan and Wolters, 2014). However, a sense of belonging within the school has also been found to be a predictor of academic success (Gillen-O'Neel and Fuligni, 2012), and I can't help but wonder what damage might be done by focusing positive messages towards 70% of a cohort, inevitably crushing the motivation and sense of belonging that the other 30% might once have felt.

Most of us carry a sense of realism about what we can and cannot achieve, but this can be skewed so easily. This is a concern I have with assemblies about heroic figures, especially those who have overcome extreme adversity and gone on to great achievements. For most mere mortals, these figures do not represent us; their experiences are often beyond our own reality, perhaps even beyond our contemplation. And for maladaptive perfectionists (Hill, 2017), these models of excellence might have serious detrimental effects on self-esteem and motivation.

My argument, then, is that assemblies and form time messages need to be considered, cohesive and consistent. Furthermore, any key messages need to be repeated and revisited in order to secure them in long-term memory, à la Rosenshine and CLT. Messages in this week's assembly should have a clear connection with messages in last week's assembly. Messages in form time should link back to messages in prior learning. In her talk given at CurriculumEd2019 in Lichfield, Sealy (2019) offers a description of curriculum as box set. This includes the notion of using *previously* … as an easy method for connecting to prior learning, and *next time* … for giving a clear sense of progression. This could be applied to PSHE education or form sessions - and assemblies too, of course - helping students to see the progressions and golden threads that run through the school's pastoral curriculum. The questions for pastoral leaders then must be:

- What is the curriculum of your assemblies?
- What is the curriculum of your form times?
- How do these connect with each other?
- How might these connect with PSHE education and/or SMSC and/or citizenship?

The Book of Common Prayer and the Golden Rule

In my current setting, the curriculum for our assemblies is pretty easy - we already have it laid out in the form of the Book of Common Prayer. Our school chaplain uses this in our weekly whole-school services, and it is also used in our weekly year group chapel services. For each week of the year, it gives a prayer and two readings - one of which is taken from the Gospels. It is the Gospel reading that we use in our assemblies. The school chaplain also identifies a theme and a relevant hymn for each week. As head of year, I lead a chapel service each week, but form tutors are also welcome to lead them. Using the Book of Common Prayer gives us a clear structure for each chapel assembly: greeting, prayer, hymn, reading, sermon (we call this the talky bit), prayer and dismissal. I try to use the talky bit to identify a relevance to the reading, linking it to our everyday experience. Luke 2:41-52 is a great example. Mary and Joseph accidentally leave a pre-teen Jesus in Jerusalem, assuming him to be in their group. When they realise, they go back and spend three days searching for him, before finding Jesus in the temple deep in discussion with the scholars, listening to them and asking questions. When his parents admonish him, Jesus asks why they needed to search - surely it would be obvious that he would be 'about [his] father's business'? In my assemblies, I draw out the message that scholarly activity is 'the father's business' but that this is more than simply building knowledge - it is the quest for wisdom. There is an obvious connection here with school, where we would hope our students might immerse themselves in active learning - listening and asking questions - in a quest for wisdom.

However, we do alter weekly chapel assemblies to suit, depending on what is happening that week. For instance, a member of SLT may wish to lead an assembly on an issue of topical importance; a group of students may wish to lead an assembly on a charity event that they are organising; a colleague may wish to promote an extracurricular activity, and so on. However, I always ensure that we end the chapel assembly with the same key message that has become something of a motto for my year groups. But I will come back to that shortly.

So, the Book of Common Prayer gives us a structured curriculum for our assemblies. And, of course, the readings and themes contain lessons. These are inevitably rooted in the Christian tradition, but we are always keen to point out that, more often than not, these lessons carry universal messages - messages which can be found in most, if not all, the major religions of the world, and in humanist philosophy too. In the teachings of Jesus we are given two commandments: love the Lord your God (Mark 12:30-31) and love thy neighbour as thyself (Matthew 22:37-39). This second commandment - to love thy neighbour - echoes a sentiment which is found in various religions and traditions and that has become known as the Golden Rule, otherwise known as the maxim of reciprocity: treat others as you would wish to be treated (Matthew 7:12; Luke 6:31). I believe this to be a useful message which can form the crux of a pastoral curriculum which places consideration of others at the centre of our actions.

This might seem to run counter to the child-centred approach which we might expect to dominate discussions of the pastoral. Indeed, a child-centred approach to safeguarding is a requirement of statutory guidance: 'all practitioners should make sure their approach is child-centred' (Department for Education, 2019c, p. 5). However, when it comes to the messages that we want children and young people to receive and think about, I believe we must shift the focus away from the narcissistic self-centred view of the world which comes naturally to them. To use a Freudian model, we have a duty to help steer them from the id and the ego and towards an informed and knowledgeable superego. This may well reflect Biesta's socialisation, but I would also like to suggest that it is an essential part of what Biesta (2015, p. 77) calls *subjectification*, whereby 'children and young people come to exist as subjects of initiative and responsibility rather than as objects of the actions of others'.

For me, the maxim of reciprocity is the perfect tool for developing a clear sense of others in students' minds. I often use the example of holding doors open, creating anecdotes about people struggling with prams, wheelchairs, walking sticks and so on: the act of holding a door open can make a big difference to someone's day. Equally, the power of saying 'thank you' to acknowledge when someone has done something for us (such as holding a door open!) has formed a central message of some of my assemblies. When I visited Michaela Community School in Brent, London, I was struck by the motto which I saw displayed around the place: 'Work hard. Be kind.' I have now adopted this as a motto in my year groups; as I half-jokingly commented to our school chaplain, condensing 2,000 years of Christian theology into just two words: be kind. The contemporary relevance of this can be seen in the public outpouring of grief and anger following the death of Caroline Flack, which manifested in the usage of #BeKind to highlight the potentially tragic consequences of cyberbullying and online trolling (*BBC News*, 2020). The need for kindness has also been acknowledged by the formation, in 2015, of the Be Kind Movement, a charity which, amongst other things, offers workshops for schools.[9]

The acknowledgement of the other is an important step towards empathy, and it is empathy which will inevitably save the world. Here, a knowledge-rich pastoral curriculum might encompass ideas of *phronesis* – practical wisdom or, better still, practical virtue.

---

9   See https://www.bekindmovement.co.uk/.

Self-Knowledge

Having shunned 'child-centred' thinking about curriculum in favour of other-centred thinking, I now wish to reassert the importance of self-knowledge. Often, children and teenagers fall foul of their own biology, reacting to situations in ways that even they do not understand. After such incidents, we may foolishly ask them, 'Why did you do that?' and then get frustrated when they reply, 'Dunno.' But what if they genuinely do not know why they have done whatever it is that they have done? Research into brain development reveals that whilst media headlines about teenagers' lack of self-control are inevitably and unhelpfully exaggerated, 'in emotional contexts, adolescents' impulse-control ability is severely taxed relative to that of children and adults' (Casey and Caudle, 2013, p. 86). However, there are a large number of variables, beyond the biological, in the lives of adolescents that might impede rational thinking about actions (Rutter, 2015). Developing an understanding of how these processes work and their implications for the classroom would be, I suggest, a very useful step for pastoral leaders – indeed, for all teachers.

For instance, Neville (2013, p. 22) shows how emotions play a significant part in cognition and brain development, concluding that 'Emotions shape both what our students see and hear and the ways they process it. We need to pay attention'. Once we have an understanding of the role of emotions in both brain development and in the ways in which we respond to situations, we might be able to develop teachable knowledge content. If our students can understand how their actions and reactions might be adversely affected by their biology, and by their own emotions, they might then be able to develop strategies of their own to ameliorate negative or maladaptive responses. Teaching children and young people to recognise their own feelings, and the feelings of others, can equip them with powerful knowledge that might enable processes of conflict resolution – a topic which will be explored in more detail in Chapter 4.

Ideas around self-knowledge echo the fascinating concept of *Bildung*, which refers to the German tradition of self-cultivation we discussed in Chapter 2. Any teacher of English should be able to tell you about the literary tradition of the *Bildungsroman* – a story which charts an experience of self-development, a coming-of-age novel. But the concept of *Bildung* carries significant potential to help unhide the pastoral curriculum, as it chimes well with ideas around character education which I explore in Chapter 7.

Conclusion

Unlike domain-specific, disciplinary subjects, the pastoral curriculum covers a diverse set of issues and approaches. Through PSHE education, citizenship and SMSC, we can see various attempts to qualify aspects of personal development, with clear curricular outcomes in the form of schemes of work in PSHE education and citizenship, with a GCSE available in the latter. However, there remains a hidden curriculum of social practices and expectations which teachers and students alike must navigate. My plea is for teachers and school leaders to think carefully about what this curriculum might be, to make it *un*hidden and to be consistent in the messages that we give our students.

Whatever your pastoral curriculum turns out to be, it should obviously include PSHE education and so on. In addition, it should address whatever needs or gaps in knowledge you have identified; such identification will need to be based on various assessments but should also be flexible, able to respond to the demands of the here and now.

In addition, it is important to recognise that your school curriculum is also about your teachers – what are their ongoing training needs? What do you want your teachers to know in order for them to do their job well?

Some key takeaways might include:

- Interrogate the hidden curriculum in your school.
- Design a knowledge-rich pastoral curriculum that encompasses knowledge of the self and knowledge of others.

- Thread key messages – golden threads – through assemblies, form times and all pastoral interactions.
- Make these golden threads explicit to colleagues and students as the *un*hidden pastoral curriculum.

Chapter 4

Bullying

Introduction

Any school leader who tells you that their school has no bullying is either a liar or a fool. There should be no shame in admitting that your school has issues with bullying. Indeed, I know of parents who would see such an acknowledgement as a strength. A police officer friend of mine told me that given a choice of two schools – one which says 'we have no bullying' and the other which says 'we do have bullying and here is how we deal with it' – he would choose to send his children to the school which admits bullying and acts upon it.

Bullying exists in every school because schools are places where human beings coalesce, specifically young human beings. It appears to be part of human nature that, from time to time, people are horrible to each other. Any denial of this is simply disingenuous. Problems occur when bullying remains hidden or undisclosed. By being open and honest about it, issues around bullying become much easier to deal with and children are much more likely to open up about their experiences. In an open culture, perpetrators of bullying are less likely to reoffend. However, there is an additional difficulty around this topic, namely that the term 'bullying' can easily be applied to situations which are, in fact, not bullying. For instance, sometimes parents might claim that their child is being bullied when the set of behaviours that are taking place can't really be characterised in this way.

It may surprise you to learn that 'There is no legal definition of bullying'[1] – a situation that perhaps reflects the complexities of the topic. Indeed, much literature comments on the lack of agreed definition (e.g. Ringrose, 2008; James et al., 2011; Mishna, 2012).

---

1   See https://www.gov.uk/bullying-at-school/bullying-a-definition.

Despite this lack of a legal definition of bullying, the Gov.uk website defines it is as behaviour that is:

- repeated
- intended to hurt someone either physically or emotionally
- often aimed at certain groups, for example because of race, religion, gender or sexual orientation

Bullying takes many forms and can include:

- physical assault
- teasing
- making threats
- name calling
- cyberbullying – bullying via mobile phone or online (for example email, social networks and instant messenger)

It is important to note that 'By law, all state (not private) schools must have a behaviour policy in place that includes measures to prevent all forms of bullying among pupils',[2] and the vast majority of schools will have an anti-bullying policy. With this being the case, what research might exist on this topic that could be used to inform such policies and, more importantly, the daily practice of dealing with incidents of bullying? A search of the journal *Pastoral Care in Education* for the word 'bullying' yields over 1,000 results, offering a range of perspectives on the issue, including results from various interventions and an exploration of coping strategies used by victims of bullying. This is a rich vein of material to call upon and it seems shocking, if unsurprising, that schools are not routinely engaged in using these resources to inform policy and practice.

---

2 See https://www.gov.uk/bullying-at-school.

This chapter is not intended to be a fully comprehensive review of the diverse literature, nor a complete guide to bullying or interventions – there are such texts in circulation (for example, Mishna, 2012). Rather, its aims are: to outline some key ideas that might inform policy and practice; to signpost you to some sources of research and information; and to ask how this might help to build a knowledge-rich pastoral curriculum in schools.

Conflict and Relational Bullying

One of the aspects of the literature that directly informed my practice was the discussion of the language used to describe and discuss those situations which might not be bullying but are certainly hostile social interactions. For some schools, such incidents are logged as 'friendship issues', but this term seems inappropriate in many cases: the children involved have never been friends and are not likely to become friends as a result of any intervention offered by teachers. Rather, these situations are better described as 'conflict'. Winslade and Williams (2012) describe conflict as 'ordinary' and, within the context of a school, 'inevitable'. Whilst the linguistic distinction may seem petty, it is in fact extremely useful in those situations in which two (or more) parties are guilty of unpleasantness. Often, incidents of 'bullying' turn out to be a cycle of conflict, in which each party feels aggrieved and like they should claim the label of 'victim' whilst casting the other in the role of 'bully'. Being able to record these incidents as such is crucial in maintaining a professional distance, showing an unbiased response to the situation. However, if, by logging each incident of 'conflict', certain names emerge as repeat participants, then a pattern of behaviour begins to emerge.

This use of language also enables a shift in how the situation is discussed with the children. Rather than taking an accusatory tone by labelling one child as the perpetrator, it is possible to view them both as participants in a conflict: both parties can be perceived as being hurt by events and both can be seen as responsible for causing hurt. Here we might look to strategies from restorative practice to restore damaged relationships between children, or at least to bring closure to the unpleasant situation. We might not expect the participants to ever become friends, but that is not really the goal: the goal is to bring an end to the conflict.

Of course, in cases in which the behaviour can be described as bullying, it is important to be clear about this with those involved. In these situations, we do not want the victim to feel that they are being blamed, and the perpetrator must be made aware of their role. Often, children do not see themselves as bullies (Ringrose, 2008), and it might require some careful navigation to enable them to see their role for what it is. This realisation can be quite disconcerting. In one case I dealt with, the perpetrators were convinced that their victim had initially played along, and were surprised when she then reacted emotionally and retaliated. Through discussion with the perpetuators I was able to show them how victims may often react in surprising ways, such as initially laughing along as a defence mechanism.

Ringrose (2008, p. 510) highlights the complexities of conflict and bullying amongst teenage girls, and the hidden psychological effects: there are higher rates of self-harm for girls than boys, girls' 'internalised' responses are harder for schools to detect or address, and there is a lack of professional understanding of gender differences in bullying, meaning that schools are not addressing girls' needs. However, Ringrose also cautions that anti-bullying policies are premised upon psychological approaches to girls' aggression, 'largely ignoring the literature on the "socio-cultural dimensions" of bullying and aggression, which argues girls' conflicts are organized through social hierarchies and structural/discursive power' (p. 511).

Ringrose is right to conclude that 'further research is needed to explore the limitations and possibilities of school anti-bullying interventions for working with girls' (p. 519). Sadly, this provides little advice for schools in how to respond to the complexities of such conflicts. However, a recognition that relational bullying is more common amongst girls (Levine and Tamburrino, 2014) would at least be the first step in helping to identify when it may be occurring.

Relational bullying takes place 'when indirect actions such as exclusion, control of peer relationships or a detachment of friendships occur' (Levine and Tamburrino, 2014, p. 272). As has already been noted, relational bullying is more common amongst girls, although it can, of course, occur amongst boys. James et al. (2011) give a useful summary of the literature describing why girls may engage in relational bullying or relational aggression. Reasons might include issues of popularity, social status, meanness and power, all of which are an expression and a source of hierarchies within groups. Further reasons include jealousy, competition and boredom. There are also various parental, familial and social influences upon relational aggression, and the possible impact of attachment difficulties. It is easy to see why James et al. suggest that 'relational aggression is not as straightforward as general bullying' (p. 441). These complexities make it very difficult to manage relational aggression: it is difficult to establish the beginning of the problem, and it can be perpetuated with different students alternating between being the perpetrator and the victim. Issues arising from relational aggression can continue into adulthood.

James et al. give the results of an intervention involving two lessons in which girls were specifically taught about relational aggression and the various issues around it. Whilst the findings were positive, the authors recognise that 'it is unrealistic to expect a two-lesson curriculum to eradicate all relational bullying' (p. 451). Given the seriousness of, and complexities involved with, the topic, such material should form part of a specific, knowledge-rich pastoral curriculum - messages around relational bullying should form a significant strand of the unhidden curriculum, be that through PSHE education or other mechanisms.

One of the biggest difficulties in identifying and tackling bullying is that of intentionality: whether or not the perpetrator intended harm. Nassem (2019, p. 25) finds that children who engage in bullying are 'usually motivated to achieve other goals such as being popular within their circle'. She also points out that individuals are not always cognisant of the difference between intentional and unintentional maltreatment. From the perspective of the victim, the intentionality might be of little consequence - they feel hurt. This is why it is important to understand the issues surrounding bullying from the perspective of the children themselves, and Nassem's book works from this premise.

Systemic Bullying

It is important to recognise the potential for systemic bullying in your setting, and the negative role that teachers can play – how teachers themselves can participate in or encourage bullying. Nassem (2020, p. 65) outlines a range of inequalities that serve to 'target children who are positioned as "vulnerable"'. For instance, many schools operate hierarchical structures based on perceived ability – streams or sets. Many of us will recall from our teacher training the concepts of labelling and self-fulfilling prophecies, and these can also be seen in the light of the Pygmalion effect and its theoretical sibling the Golem effect (Rosenthal and Jacobson, 1968; Babad et al., 1982; Didau, 2015). Teachers subconsciously treat those students who they perceive as 'bright' or 'dull' differently: 'thick' is a particularly pernicious, and cruel, label that children often bear for many years having 'internalized' it (Nassem, 2020, p. 67). Similarly, those who have been labelled 'naughty' are treated differently. The 'thick' kids and the 'naughty' kids are placed under surveillance as teachers 'are required as part of their role to monitor the behaviour and performance' of such children (p. 66).

Furthermore, such labels lead to marginalising uses of language. For instance, Nassem refers to a private school where teachers refer to those in the lowest stream as 'the diddlydonks' (p. 67). Anecdotally, we have probably all heard teachers in the staffroom referring to children in all sorts of unpleasant terms. Even in meetings, colleagues might speak with disdain about those students who have been identified as troublesome. I'm sure that I have fallen into this trap myself from time to time. Linguists will tell you that there is a strong correlation between language and thought, and that the words we use to talk about something can affect the way we think about it. Therefore, if we typically use negative, derogatory language in our discourse about children in the staffroom or in meetings, then we are likely to foster a culture of negativity throughout our school. The way in which we speak to and about children in the classroom will filter through to the corridors, the dining room, the playground and the dark, shadowy unsupervised areas of the school - the toilets, the corner of the field, the bus and so on.

But even without the cruelty of labelling, teachers can unwittingly contribute to bullying either by ignoring 'banter' in the classroom or by engaging in it themselves. Of course, joviality can be an important element in forming good rapport with students, but teachers must take great care not to engage in humiliation. Nassem shows how some children feel singled out and unfairly punished for a range of minor, even petty, matters; and that children felt distressed by being shouted at by teachers, which was a fairly common occurrence.

Nassem goes on to discuss other important aspects of systemic bullying, such as social class and gender. With regard to the latter, she highlights issues around school uniform policies which insist that girls wear skirts, citing Foucault's *Discipline and Punish* in her observation that girls' bodies are 'objects of control and manipulation' (p. 75), making some girls feel 'vulnerable to sexual abuse' (p. 85). This would be an unintended consequence of school policy, and it makes me wonder how many of our policies and practices have other such unintended consequences and how we might go about trying to identify them.

It is clearly important, therefore, to create a culture which encourages genuine student voice and allows students agency. School leaders must engage with ongoing policy and practice review, which reflects upon the daily experiences of all children and seeks to eliminate discriminatory discourse and actions. For instance, Nassem observes that even classroom displays could contribute to children feeling victimised - postcards bearing the legend 'boys who read are superior beings' potentially reinforced negative perceptions of those with literacy difficulties (p. 69).

Cyberbullying

A large proportion of contemporary pastoral issues are exacerbated by digital technology: in particular, social media and messaging apps mean that issues, arguments and gossip continue well beyond the school gates. Most of the pastoral issues that I encounter revolve around breakdowns in social relations between students, and these often involve WhatsApp groups in which students continue to talk about issues that could otherwise have been resolved. What makes it worse, of course, is when students are booted out of these groups or when new groups are created which exclude particular individuals. Children probe each other about what has happened or been said, or share third-hand bits of gossip with each other. There are screenshots swapped and photographs of sad faces. And, of course, it is impossible to properly read tone in the messages that we receive in this medium. Another aspect which makes the technology pernicious is the always-on nature of the devices, with notifications pinging and demanding attention throughout the night. When I tell my students the age restrictions on various apps, they are often surprised – you must be 16 to use WhatsApp,[3] despite what it says in the Apple app store; 18 for a YouTube channel (13 with parental consent). Parents often do not know these age limits either. I have now taken to writing to all parents at the start of each term with a reminder, and I include the information as part of our welcome evening presentations to parents in early September.

Social media apps are a haven for relational bullying. They represent an adult-free space, a disturbing heterotopia, a digital playground in which the hidden curriculum is written, delivered and made explicit by children who seem to take turns in wielding power – and bullying is all about power. And just as playground bullying involves participants occupying different roles, so too does cyberbullying (Betts et al., 2016). Most children seem to have an understanding of bullying in the 'real world' of the playground or changing rooms, at least when it comes to physical bullying, name calling and so on. However, when it comes to what's said and

---

3 See https://faq.whatsapp.com/en/iphone/26000151/.

shared in online spaces, children's recognition of bullying behaviours seems limited. For instance, it is often perceived that bullying is a repeated behaviour (as we saw in the definition offered by the Gov.uk website). A child may post a comment on an online forum or social network and not fully appreciate that this might be reposted, retweeted or otherwise shared. In this case, the comment has been repeated from the perspective of the victim. Meanwhile, students who see unpleasant comments being made about a peer in a WhatsApp group become bystanders.

There is a growing concern about the role of the bystander in cases of bullying, and increasing calls for bystanders to take action - either by stepping in or by reporting the bullying. However, Nassem (2019) cautions that issues around bystanders may be more complex than that. For instance, even teachers and school norms can reinforce the ostracisation of certain students, thus restricting the agency of individuals. Indeed, Nassem sees the bystander as caught up in complex power dynamics within groups.

Whilst Nassem's observations about the complex dynamics of bystanding are grounded in the institutional practices of the school, they nonetheless have significance when discussing cyberbullying. It is easy for us as adults outside of the site of interaction to insist that children report any unpleasantness that they observe in online spaces. But the reality for those embroiled in the situation is not 'virtual' - it is manifestly actual. All of the dynamics of playground bullying are in play in these online spaces. For instance, they fear reporting incidents of online bullying behaviours just as much as reporting incidents of offline bullying. It is often suggested that children should take screenshots of unpleasant comments received via Snapchat, but that might exacerbate the problem as the sender receives a notification when a screenshot is taken, fuelling accusations of being a 'grass'. This kind of fear would inevitably cause a reticence to speak out. As pastoral leaders, we need to be much more aware of the various complexities of these online exchanges. It is not enough to simply say, 'They shouldn't be using these apps', or that it is the responsibility of parents to police their children's online behaviour. We need to be alert to our students' use of these technologies - which can often take place within as well as beyond the school gates - and we must adopt a proactive approach to teaching students about the impact they have in online spaces, and about the nature of cyberbullying.

Intervention Strategies

Sadly, there seems to be very little useful advice for teachers and school leaders about how to effectively respond to incidents of bullying. There are mixed messages in the literature about which interventions are most likely to be effective (Ringrose, 2008; James et al., 2011; Mishna, 2012; Winslade and Williams, 2012; Espelage et al., 2013). However, adopting a whole-school approach has certainly been found to be effective, when issues around bullying are incorporated into the curriculum and discussed in lessons. This should be a feature of a knowledge-rich pastoral curriculum and should form one of the golden threads that run through the unhidden curriculum. Students should be taught about bullying in their PSHE education lessons: they should learn the definitions of bullying, cyberbullying and bystanding as well as learning the difference between bullying and conflict. They should be taught to recognise the signs of bullying and encouraged to speak out and report any incidents that they witness.

The Department for Education (2017, p. 10) tells us that 'Schools which excel at tackling bullying have created an ethos of good behaviour where pupils treat one another and the school staff with respect because they know that this is the right way to behave'. This guidance document also bullet-points strategies employed by 'successful' schools, such as involving parents and students in discussions about bullying and making sure that all are clear about the school anti-bullying policy. Successful schools also 'provide effective staff training' so that 'all school staff understand the principles and purpose of the school's policy, its legal responsibilities regarding bullying, how to resolve problems, and where to seek support' (p. 11). Sadly, the guidance does not extend to suggestions for how staff might go about resolving problems. However, it does make clear that successful schools 'implement disciplinary sanctions. The consequences of bullying reflect the seriousness of the incident so that others see that bullying is unacceptable' (p. 11).

In responding to incidents of bullying, it might be tempting to adopt approaches such as restorative practice or mediation. However, whilst these might be appropriate in cases of relational conflict, they may not be suitable when it comes to bullying. Because bullying involves power dynamics, such strategies may in fact be harmful (Dupper, 2013). This is why it is essential that teachers and pastoral leaders are clear about what they are dealing with – whether the current case is one of conflict or whether it is bullying. Being clear about the distinction is important and should be a feature of CPD and part of the school's knowledge-rich pastoral curriculum for students and for staff. It is also important that incidents are recorded centrally, with brief but accurate comments about what happened and the names of all those present – including bystanders.

In pragmatic praxis, then, how can we deal with incidents of bullying? I would suggest that it is necessary to foster an anti-bullying school culture, using a knowledge-rich pastoral curriculum to teach students, staff and parents about bullying and conflict. It is vital that incidents of bullying are dealt with swiftly and that the perpetrators receive sanctions. However, perpetrators should then be provided with a package of learning to help them understand the consequences of their actions.

For instance, I once dealt with a boy who had posted unpleasant comments about another boy in Google reviews of local businesses. Of course, this resulted in a sanction, but it was also important that the perpetrator saw this as a learning opportunity. He received detentions, during which we discussed the nature of bullying and cyberbullying, including the potential impact and consequences. The perpetrator was mortified to realise that his actions in fact met the criteria for cyberbullying, because the comments were malicious and repeated. It was important that he saw the situation from the outside – as an observer, so to speak.

In similar instances, I have used the wonderful power of stick figures drawn to depict each of the participants in the scenario, labelling them A, B and so on. It is fairly easy for the children to see which one is them, but it enables the conversation to occur without a sense of personal judgement coming from me. I then describe the patterns of behaviour as being 'consistent with the criteria of bullying', so that I am not calling an individual a bully, but rather identifying the behaviour as bullying. In the case of cyberbullying, I show perpetrators the definitions at Bullying UK and simply ask them to identify which behaviours they recognise.[4] Nassem (2019) suggests that developing interventions which reflect students' own experiences is likely to be more effective than those of fictional characters.

Nassem is also keen to point out that children want teachers to take bullying more seriously. She gives the example of a student who had reported bullying but no action was taken, so she 'had to sit in the same lessons as the people who bullied her which paralysed her with terror' (p. 57). Nassem then explores the potential problems with placing children in different classes, if only temporarily - not as a punishment, but as a step towards a resolution. Through ongoing discussion with the children involved, it might be possible for them to eventually return to lessons together. Here Nassem advocates bringing the children together to discuss their issues and agree upon ways to move forward. These 'development meetings' form a core part of the strategies that Nassem puts forward. She outlines a holistic approach which, in the main, seems very sensible. It takes account of different forms of bullying, including institutional aspects that I had perhaps not fully considered before. Furthermore, she raises important questions about school culture which all school leaders would benefit from considering.

Conclusion

Whilst there are no simple answers to the question of how to deal with bullying, it is clear that schools need to develop a consistent and robust set of protocols for responding to incidents. In order to do this, pastoral leaders need to establish clear working definitions of key terms - bullying, conflict, bystander, etc. - to distinguish

---

4 See https://www.bullying.co.uk/cyberbullying/what-is-cyberbullying.

between different behaviours and provide a language with which to accurately discuss these issues. Bullying should be a topic within a strong, knowledge-rich pastoral curriculum.

Key recommendations might include:

- Establish a strong anti-bullying culture that engages students and adults in open discussion about what constitutes bullying and ways in which students experience it.
- Give students clear guidance on how to report incidents of bullying.
- Think very carefully about the institutional messages that children receive and aim to tackle institutional discrimination.
- Respond swiftly to incidents of bullying, employing clear consequences but also development meetings, mentoring and coaching.
- Have clear working definitions for conflict and bullying, and use these definitions when recording incidents.
- Ensure that records include the names of all participants – notably bystanders.
- Include specific training for teachers about conflict and bullying as part of ongoing CPD.
- Deliver specific lessons on friendships, conflict and bullying in your pastoral curriculum.
- Develop informative materials for parents around the issues of bullying and conflict.

Most importantly, pastoral leaders need to actively engage with the topic to develop informed policies and approaches.

Chapter 5

Wellbeing, Mental Health and Attachment

Introduction

There are growing concerns in the popular educational discourse around both children's and teachers' mental health and wellbeing. On the one hand, we see frequent reports of children and young people experiencing increasingly worrying mental ill health, often attributed to their time in school as well as the negative impact of social media. On the other hand, we read of the struggles that schools face in retaining teachers and we can see from various emotionally charged television adverts that teacher recruitment is equally difficult. Each of these situations is regularly referred to as a 'crisis'.

It is difficult to ascertain whether the apparent rise in mental health problems amongst young people reflects an increase in incidence or an increase in diagnosis, reporting and general recognition of symptoms. In 2017 the NHS found a 'slight increase over time in the prevalence of mental disorder in 5 to 15 year olds' (NHS Digital, 2018). The numbers were, according to Professor Tamsin Ford, '"not huge, not the epidemic you see reported"', despite the fact that the number of children seeking help from CAMHS had 'more than doubled over the past two years' (Schraer, 2019b). There appears to be a disparity: a rise in self-reported conditions, but no 'equivalent rise in the numbers showing signs of psychological distress when given a formal psychiatric assessment' (Schraer, 2019b). Schraer suggests that this disparity might reflect children and their parents being better able to recognise difficulties: various mental health awareness campaigns may well have had the positive impact of … raising awareness!

Nonetheless, that there has been a rise in reported mental ill health in teenagers is undeniable. Whilst many commentators point to social media as playing a significant part in this, it would be disingenuous to pretend that schools are entirely blame free. As one young reporter points out, the education system puts great pressure on teenagers to perform academically, and ultimately generates a sense of dread for the future: 'Universities as well as schools repeatedly tell teenagers that we are not good enough because our grades are not good enough, and no matter how hard we try, we're taught that any perceived academic failure could affect the rest of our lives' (McCarthy, 2019). This personal account echoes many concerns expressed elsewhere around the data-based, target-driven examination culture that is perceived to permeate the UK education system. Different commentators point to Gove's GCSE reforms, Ofsted judgements, league tables and so on. I suspect that these are easy scapegoats, and that some senior leaders may well be generating some of the pressure felt in schools out of their own fear of the consequences of poor results on their own careers. I've heard stories of Year 6 children being expected to attend SATs 'revision' classes during their Easter holidays. This is deranged. My own daughters' school does a residential trip to Paris during term time instead. This seems a much better way of helping 10-year-olds to prepare for SATs in my mind – a cultural learning experience well beyond the narrow confines of Key Stage 2 examinations, giving the children positive memories that they will carry with them into adulthood.

Meanwhile, as the mental health crisis unfolds, 'One in four children and young people referred to mental health services in England last year were not accepted for treatment' (Weale, 2020a). Apparently, treatment was refused on the grounds that 'children's conditions were not suitable, or were not serious enough to meet the threshold' (Weale, 2020a). The inevitable question then follows: what happens to these children? Must they simply wait for symptoms to worsen before they can get help?

There is clearly a need for schools to think about student mental health by asking three equally important questions:

1 In what ways are we supporting students' mental health?
2 In what ways might we be contributing to students' mental ill health?

3   What can we do better?

The Role of Schools

As noted in Chapter 1, the Department for Education (2016, p. 6) recognises the 'crucial role' that schools can play 'in helping to support good mental health and in preventing and identifying mental health issues in children and young people'. There is a clear dual aspect here – prevention and intervention. This aligns with two of the key elements of school-based counselling identified by BACP (2015). The government's commitment to addressing youth mental health issues was reaffirmed in a joint green paper from the Department of Health and the Department for Education (2017, p. 4), which promised to 'provide children and young people with an unprecedented level of support to tackle early signs of mental health issues' with an approach consisting of three key elements:

1   Incentivising every school to identify a DSLMH.
2   Funding new mental health support teams.
3   Trialling a four-week waiting period for access to specialist mental health services.

For schools, the first of these is particularly significant. I hope that all schools embrace this new role: having a designated mental health lead will help them to interrogate their policies and practice to ensure that the second of my key questions is being addressed: in what ways might we be contributing to students' mental ill health? The holder of this role would act as a crucial advocate for students. The green paper is clear that the DSLMH should also act as a link between schools and other services to 'provide rapid advice, consultation and signposting' (p. 4). In order for this role to be effective, the green paper recognises the need for specific training, and it insists that 'We will ensure that a member of staff in every primary and secondary school receives mental health awareness training' (p. 5).

The green paper goes on to claim that 'Nearly half of schools and colleges already have specific mental health leads' (p. 19). This is a claim that I find difficult to recognise in my own experience of working in schools, so I ran a poll on Twitter, which revealed that 35.9% of respondents' schools did have a specific mental health lead, whilst 64.1% did not.[1] This poll only received 295 votes, so I can't claim that it is a truly representative sample! Even so, I was pleasantly surprised by the suggestion that even a third of schools do have a member of staff leading on mental health. What was unclear was whether or not they held this role in addition to other duties.

What is essential to the success of such a role is, of course, time. A concern might be that schools award the title of mental health lead to a keen member of staff without investing properly in either the training or the directed time necessary for that person to make a significant impact. However, the schools would still be able to claim that action has been taken because, 'Hey, we have a mental health lead.'

The green paper also commits to developing mental health and wellbeing as part of the curriculum through PSHE education. Indeed, this commitment was echoed in 2019 when the Department for Education announced that 'All students will be taught about mental and physical wellbeing' from September 2020 as part of the push for schools to deliver health education across all phases, relationships education for primary students, and RSE for secondary students (Department for Education and Hinds, 2019a). This is codified in (draft) statutory guidance which outlines the content which is to be delivered in different phases (Department for Education, 2019e).

With this increased focus on the importance of mental health awareness and intervention in schools, teachers and school leaders will be seeking resources to assist in their delivery of this new element of the curriculum. The PSHE Association offers guidance on teaching about mental health and wellbeing, along with teaching resources such as lesson plans and associated PowerPoint

---

1   Twitter poll, 11 January 2020. Available at: https://twitter.com/sputniksteve/status/1216128507056664578?s=20.

slides.[2] Whilst some of these can only be accessed by members, some are freely available.

Raines (2019, p. 1) offers evidence-based approaches to addressing mental health issues in schools, acknowledging that 'schools have become the default mental health providers for children and adolescents'. Whilst his focus is on US schools, where it is possible to find school-employed mental health practitioners who are state licensed or state certified, his book might nonetheless offer UK school leaders useful information with regard to a range of mental health issues that students may face.

Glazzard and Bancroft (2018) provide a useful set of tools to assist schools in developing an informed approach to mental health issues. Their book outlines key risk factors and provides guidance on identifying and supporting young people with a range of issues, such as anxiety and depression, conduct disorders, self-harm, LGBT+ related concerns, and so on. With the increased governmental focus on addressing mental health issues in schools, I hope that more resources like this will soon follow.

Sadfishing and Social Media

Amid growing concerns about the mental ill health of children and adolescents, there have been particular alarms raised about a disturbing trend known as 'sadfishing', in which young people use social media to make '"exaggerated claims about their emotional problems to generate sympathy"' (Coughlan, 2019b). This, inevitably, makes it even more difficult for young people who are facing genuine mental health issues to get help, due to a reluctance to speak up for fear of being accused of attention seeking.

Underlying this phenomenon is the fact that young people are increasingly turning to online platforms to express their distress, rather than speaking to someone in school or at home. Perhaps there is a perceived safety buffer at play: it's easier to say

---

2   See https://www.pshe-association.org.uk/curriculum-and-resources/resources/ guidance-teaching-about-mental-health-and.

something from behind a screen than it is to say it face to face (a factor that causes a good deal of trouble with social media generally!). These apparently attention-seeking pleas for help are perhaps a crucial outlet for young people (and, indeed, adults). Within the edu-Twitter community I have seen a number of tweets which seem to be cries for help, with the community rallying around to offer support. However, this use of the platform can be a cynical ploy by influencers to gain followers and build a brand (Jargon, 2019). Young people who see this kind of online behaviour may be encouraged to follow suit, using social media to articulate their mental health issues and thus gaining support from peers and strangers alike.

However, this form of disclosure can open them up to accusations of sadfishing and make them more likely to be victims of cyberbullying, which could spill over into the real world of daily school interactions. Imagine the scenario: a teen posts on Instagram that they are feeling depressed, anxious or even suicidal because of bullying at school. The next day, they find that the post has been shared around the school by their peers, and the bullying intensifies.

It seems that adolescents who spend three or more hours per day on social media 'may be at heightened risk for mental health problems, particularly internalizing problems' (Riehm et al., 2019, p. 1266). Furthermore, the nature of social media activity both appeals to adolescents and risks influencing their behaviour, for good or ill. Teenage brain development is understood to leave individuals prone to peer influences, which plays out online as well as in face-to-face social settings. The behaviour of friends can significantly promote the adoption of risky behaviours that are detrimental to mental health, but this is also true of the behaviour of friends of friends of friends – 'up to three or more degrees of separation' (Lamblin et al., 2017, p. 61). Young people tend to be more susceptible to online influence than adults, and social media can increase a teenager's exposure to risk-taking behaviours which appear normalised amongst peers. However, as Lamblin et al. point out, social media could also offer 'new opportunities for treatment and intervention in adolescent mental health' (p. 64) through the development of new apps and the tailoring of online social networks to provide an alternative to traditional therapies. However, 'Given that social media helps to normalize adolescent moods and behaviors, ensuring that teens are exposed to reliable information, positive influences and supportive environments within their online worlds can promote resilience and mental well-being' (p. 64).

For schools, it is important to develop a good understanding of the psychology involved in teen social media use, as well as of brain development and how this can impact on mental health and wellbeing – especially at a time of increasing pressure from school workload, GCSE option choices and the focus on preparing for exams. Through adopting a pragmatic approach informed by continual engagement with reliable sources of information, teachers and leaders should ensure that they are aware of the ever-developing nature of social media and its appeal to adolescents and young people. The latest craze of children using TikTok is another reminder that age restrictions on social media apps have very little enforceability. Whilst TikTok has an age rating of 12+ in the Apple app store, and an age limit of 13 in the company's terms and conditions,[3] younger children are using it to film and upload videos of themselves, which can be viewed by anyone, dependent upon the account settings. We must be alert to the ways in which children and teenagers can potentially make themselves vulnerable through these technologies.

But we must also ensure that our knowledge-rich pastoral curriculum includes as many opportunities as possible to discuss the online world with our students, engaging with them to discover what apps they are using and guiding them to sources of reliable information about appropriate usage.[4] Social media has an overwhelming appeal, and we won't be able to stop young people accessing and using it. So we must help them to understand it, and to develop strategies for keeping themselves and their peers safe.

---

3   See https://www.tiktok.com/legal/terms-of-use?lang=en#terms-eea.

4   For example: https://www.bbc.co.uk/cbbc/findoutmore/help-me-out-staying-safe-online; https://www.childline.org.uk/info-advice/bullying-abuse-safety/online-mobile-safety/staying-safe-online/; http://www.safetynetkids.org.uk/personal-safety/staying-safe-online/; and https://www.bullying.co.uk/cyberbullying/how-to-stay-safe-online/.

Direct Instruction, Project Follow Through, Self-Esteem and Praise

It may seem strange to have a section about direct instruction in a chapter about wellbeing and mental health. However, I think that the startling results of the horribly named Project Follow Through have ramifications for our discussion here. Project Follow Through was the largest education experiment ever conducted, and it took place in the USA during the 1960s and 1970s. The project measured a range of education programmes against measures of academic attainment, self-esteem and problem solving. As the website for National Institute for Direct Instruction (NIDI) states: 'The results were strong and clear. Students who received Direct Instruction had significantly higher academic achievement than students in any of the other programs. They also had higher self esteem and self-confidence.'[5]

I am not going to mount an argument here for the highly scripted lessons involved in Engelmann's model of Direct Instruction – in capitals here as it refers specifically to the Engelmann model – as promoted by NIDI, but it is important to note the high impact that the Direct Instruction programme had on students' self-esteem, especially when programmes which were specifically designed to improve self-esteem had little – or sometimes even a negative – impact upon that very measure. In other words, programmes designed to improve self-esteem failed, whilst Direct Instruction – which was targeting improvement in academic outcomes – had the largest positive impact upon academic measures *and* self-esteem. The implications of this finding for schools are clear: if we want students to have high self-esteem, then we must do all that we can to give them experiences of academic success from an early age. There is clearly a link between self-esteem and good mental health. Given what we have already said about teenage brain development, and what we know from observing how teenagers develop socially and emotionally, it is vital that we provide children with academic success before they hit those troublesome teenage years. It is equally important to ensure that teenagers are given the

---

5 See https://www.nifdi.org/what-is-di/project-follow-through.

opportunity to succeed academically as they move through Key Stages 3 and 4 in order to make the transition as smooth as possible.

For many students, academic success may not be a significant feature of their school experience. Too often, students can be left feeling as though they are stupid, either in particular subjects or across the board. There is a whole field of work that we could explore here around the negative effects of setting (Hattie, 2008), the Golem effect (Babad et al., 1982) and the self-fulfilling prophecy, but suffice it to say that there are clear, and somewhat obvious, correlations between poor academic outcomes and poor self-esteem that – regardless of the direction of causality – are worth acknowledging. It is therefore important that heads of year and pastoral leaders take a keen interest in students' academic success and progress. Most job descriptions acknowledge this as an important part of the role.

Intervention programmes are typically provided for students in Year 11 who find themselves falling below their target grades, but I wonder about the extent to which similar interventions are conducted for students in Key Stage 3. Where they are, what data is used to identify students who might need the intervention? I'm very uneasy around any kind of target grading. In my context, teachers are asked to provide half-termly data on attainment and attitude to learning (ATL), and our interventions are based upon ATL scores. We employ a range of strategies, mostly following a coaching approach that develops along bespoke lines depending upon the identified needs of the student. If we can help students to cultivate a more proactive and positive ATL in Key Stage 3, then perhaps they will not need the extensive academic intervention that would come in Year 11. In any case, an effective intervention and mentoring programme should seek to acknowledge the link between self-esteem and academic success.

But, equally, it is important for class teachers to acknowledge the positive impact on wellbeing and self-esteem that can be wrought by academic success, as indicated by Project Follow Through. Crucially, this need not be solely related to test scores. In an average day, there are potentially hundreds of opportunities for teachers to create positive academic encounters: little successes in the smallest moments of the lesson.

In his increasingly popular paper, upon which an entire education publication industry appears to have rapidly been built, Rosenshine (2012, p. 17) highlights the importance of students obtaining a 'high success rate during classroom instruction'. This is to ensure that errors are not repeated, and thus that correct information is secured in long-term memory. He tells us that the research 'suggests that the optimal success rate for fostering student achievement appears to be about 80 percent' (p. 17). When Rosenshine talks of things being optimal, he is talking about the optimal conditions for learning – a high success rate in lessons leads to higher long-term retention of material. Rosenshine does not talk about self-esteem. However, it is obvious that these small classroom successes, if acknowledged by the teacher, will have a positive impact on self-esteem and wellbeing. A verbal acknowledgement of the success might give the student a positive view of the encounter, a sense of recognition and, more importantly, a sense of achievement.

I need to be careful here though. Didau (2015) outlines a range of problems with giving praise, citing Kohn and Hattie along the way. He points out that studies show how teachers' use of praise can have minimal, or even a negative, impact upon learning. Meanwhile, Kohn (2012) suggests that 'praising them for the effort they've made can also backfire: It may communicate that they're really not very capable and therefore unlikely to succeed at future tasks'. Of course, Kohn (2018) wrote an entire book about why rewards are a bad thing, which recently enjoyed a 25th anniversary edition. His basic thesis is that rewards are a function of authoritarian adult control and that they ultimately do not work. Elsewhere, Kohn (2005) has written about the necessity for children to feel unconditional love that is not predicated on the expectation (or hope) of extrinsic reward. However, praise has been found to be effective as a behaviour management intervention (Moore et al., 2019), and Dewar (2019) gives several examples of research pointing to the positive impacts of praise.

Pragmatically, as a pastoral concern, I would argue that in place of *praise* we should perhaps talk of *encouragement* – an air of unrelenting positive regard, and what Dix (2017) calls 'deliberate botheredness'. Within this, class teachers should aim to create ample opportunities for students to enjoy lots of successes in order to aid the long-term retention of information, and to recognise these successes briefly - not as praise, but as acknowledgement to aid in the consolidation of positive self-esteem.

Attachment Theory

If we were to judge solely on the dichotomous nature of edu-Twitter discourse, attachment theory is either one of the most important things that teachers should be trained on or an over-applied model that has no relevance for the vast majority of teachers or classroom settings. In pursuing a pragmatic praxis, it is necessary to explore the space between these binary positions.

Attachment theory begins with Bowlby (2005 [1979], 2008 [1988]; Holmes, 2014), who explored the early bonds formed between an infant and its primary caregiver. In normal development, the primary caregiver becomes a secure base for the infant; without this secure base, the infant is likely to become fearful and less likely to explore. The work of Bowlby was extended by Ainsworth (e.g. Ainsworth et al., 1978) and others during the final quarter of the twentieth century, with different categories of attachment disorder being identified and described. The theory maintains a significant place in psychology - for instance, a recent title considers how attachment theory can be employed to develop our understanding of psychosis (Berry et al., 2020).

What are the implications of this for teachers? Well, according to Rose (2019), there are none. In his article for researchED, he suggests that 'there's nothing a teacher can do that they shouldn't already be doing'. He points out that teachers are not in a position to diagnose attachment disorders, nor should they engage in therapy with children who may have such disorders. The strategies that they are recommended to use when dealing with such children are, according to Rose, the very same that they would employ when faced with any form of challenging behaviour.

However, Rose's argument is related to rare cases of diagnosed attachment disorders in young children and seems not to take account of more recent work on attachment that suggests it is 'important across childhood, not just in toddlerhood' (Bergin and Bergin, 2009, p. 142) and that highlights the importance of secure attachment not only to parents, but to teachers and schools. Rose (2019) warns that 'Teachers should not confuse their role in loco parentis with being the primary caregiver for a child', but that view seems to overlook more contemporary work on attachment, which reveals a much more complex relationship between teachers and students.

Riley (2011) argues that attachment is foundational in understanding human relationships, not just in children but also in adults. He states that when applied to the classroom and the staffroom, attachment theory 'helps to explain the variance in classroom behaviour by teachers, students and school leaders when other factors are accounted for' (p. 38). Riley's account of the theory around attachment raises significant implications for teachers and school leaders that could radically alter the ways in which we think about behaviour and other pastoral concerns. The dynamic interactions between teachers and students can be seen as a reciprocal attachment which Riley suggests could be called alloattachments, and an awareness of this complex relationship could be operationalised into a more pastoral-centred approach to policy and practice in terms of creating a positive school culture and dealing with issues as they arise. This includes raising school leaders' awareness of the attachment needs of their staff as a crucial element in improving their wellbeing, which would inevitably lead to an increase in student wellbeing, as teachers are secure and happy in their work. Teachers' own attachment needs, as manifested in their relationships with students, are also explored extensively by Riley and this presents an interesting perspective upon issues such as behaviour management, where a consideration of the attachment needs of the teacher might result in a modified approach.

In addition, attachment theory has potential in helping us to understand the complex interpersonal dynamics at play in relational conflict and bullying. So, as pragmatic practitioners, we should be reluctant to dismiss attachment theory out of hand. Rather, classroom teachers, pastoral leaders and senior leaders should engage with the literature on this topic and at least consider the question *what if?* What if it does offer a different lens through which to view the complex human dynamics at play in the classroom, in the corridors, on the playground, in the changing rooms and in online spaces? What might it offer in terms of developing a more nuanced approach to staff leadership? Could line managers become caregivers? Could they, indeed, become care seekers? Attachment theory is not just about the diagnosis of rare attachment disorders; it is, potentially, a useful descriptive model for understanding the complexities of the human relationships which are at the heart of our work as teachers, and the definition of our work as pastoralists.

Conclusion

The mental health and wellbeing of our students and colleagues must be our primary concern. In fact, it could be argued that this constitutes an aspect of safeguarding and should, as such, be a regular element of our praxis discourse. Senior leaders should constantly be asking 'How will this impact upon our staff?' and interrogating every policy and every initiative. And we should all be contemplating how the children and young people in our care experience school on a daily basis.

It is vital that we consider the braided nature of the academic and the pastoral to ensure that all aspects of our provision are solely focused upon ensuring that students feel safe and happy in school, so that they can attain, and that they attain so that they feel safe and happy. This is the yin and yang of schooling.

Some key suggestions might include:

- Identify a DSLMH, give them time to do the job, and equip them with specialist training that is regularly updated.
- Identify key members of staff to become mental health first aiders.

- Build a positive culture through careful and deliberate use of language, avoidance of labels, and considered deployment of praise.
- Incorporate repeated key messages about social media into your knowledge-rich pastoral curriculum.
- Consider the attachment needs of your students and staff.

Chapter 6

Behaviour

Introduction

One of the biggest topics in the discourse of education, particularly as it plays out on edu-Twitter, is that of behaviour. This is unsurprising given that the 'damaging impact of dealing with low level persistent disruption on a regular basis is one of the main reasons teachers give for leaving the profession' (Williams, 2018, p. 32). Even veteran teachers experience lessons disrupted by poor behaviour (McInerney, 2018). The discourse includes discussions about whether behaviour really is all that bad, but is dominated by arguments around the most effective ways to deal with poor behaviour. Ideas such as 'zero tolerance' and 'no excuses' are routinely criticised, whilst restorative practice is lauded; schools that use permanent exclusion are shamed, whilst others are accused of 'off-rolling'; 'silent corridors' are demonised and 'isolation booths' are the work of Satan.

Of course, these arguments are ideological – all arguments are, and don't let anyone tell you otherwise. It is difficult amongst all the heated bluster to locate any arguments that actually rest upon evidence. Even when reports appear to be grounded in data, they can still be misleading. For instance, the Steer Report (2009) claimed – based on Ofsted reports – that behaviour in most schools was good or better. However, I'd argue that this is a poor proxy for measuring actual behaviour in schools across the country, and even Ofsted officials recognise the difficulties inherent in judging behaviour through inspection (Whieldon, 2019). In 2014 Ofsted produced a report into low-level disruption called *Below the Radar*, the results of which Her Majesty's Chief Inspector (HMCI) Amanda Spielman later described as 'disturbing' (Ofsted and Spielman, 2019).

Behaviour in schools has been a major aspect of governmental review over the years, as seen in, for example, the landmark Elton

Report (Department of Education and Science, 1989) through to the recent Bennett Report (2017). The latter presents a synthesis of strategies based on observations of practice in those schools graded as good or outstanding by Ofsted, providing a research-based manifesto situated in what amounts to grounded theory. Meanwhile, the government has issued advice and guidance to schools that presents similar distillations, although without explicit acknowledgement of the basis for the suggestions.[1] Taylor (2011, p. 5) puts forward a behaviour checklist for teachers, which includes the following items:

- Know the names and roles of any adults in class.
- Meet and greet students when they come into the classroom.
- Display rules in the class – and ensure that the students and staff know what they are.
- Display the tariff of sanctions in class.
- Have a system in place to follow through with all sanctions.
- Display the tariff of rewards in class.
- Have a system in place to follow through with all rewards.
- Have a visual timetable on the wall.
- Follow the school behaviour policy.

Some of these points already look a little out of date, and I'm not sure that they would meet with universal agreement from teachers, school leaders or behaviour consultants. However, they do point towards the need for consistency within systems which, as we shall see, is a common factor in all of the approaches to behaviour management that I explore in this chapter.

---

1 See, for example, https://www.gov.uk/government/publications/behaviour-and-discipline-in-schools.

Approaches to Behaviour Management

In his survey of the literature, Hart (2010) gives an overview of elements that have been identified as contributing to effective classroom behaviour management:

- Rules.
- Reinforcement of appropriate behaviour.
- Response to undesired behaviour.
- Staff-student relationships and interactions.
- Expectations.
- Procedures for chronic misbehaviour.
- Classroom environment.

Hart also gives an account of a 'number of distinct approaches to managing behaviour with roots in psychological theory, and with markedly different emphases in relation to the choice of strategy that a teacher might use' (p. 354):

- Behavioural approaches that employ reinforcement of positive behaviours and ignore unwanted behaviours, or use time outs.
- Psychodynamic approaches based on attachment theory.
- System approaches, which focus on social interactions.
- Humanistic approaches that attach great significance to the relationship between teacher and student.

Much of the discourse on edu-Twitter expresses concern about behavioural approaches, preferring psychodynamic approaches – derived from attachment theory – which emphasise the 'importance to children of stable, caring and trusting relationships with adults' (p. 358). Behavioural approaches are frequently demonised, and guidance from the Department for Education and Ofsted criticised for adopting such approaches. For instance, the release of Bennett's (2019) summary advice for beginning teachers met with precisely these kinds of criticisms, particularly the suggestion that he tries to apply secondary school behaviourism to other sectors. Meanwhile,

Titcombe (2019) takes aim at the behaviourism of pedagogies and strategies favoured by minister of state for school standards Nick Gibb, such as CLT and Rosenshine's principles of instruction.

Whilst we should never be fooled into thinking that edu-Twitter necessarily reflects anything other than its own bubble, the criticisms of behaviourism seen in the online discourse echo 'misgivings' found by Hart (2010) in his survey of the literature. Concerns include the fear that the use of rewards might have a negative impact upon intrinsic motivation: a fear that experimental studies suggest is actually 'unfounded', suggesting that verbal rewards increase intrinsic motivation. Having no evidential proof of harm, criticisms then become more ideological: rewards are coercive and behavioural approaches provide 'reactive and quick-fix solutions' (p. 357).

However, despite these criticisms, it seems that behavioural approaches are generally favoured by educational psychologists. Hart finds that the most popular strategies amongst educational psychologists 'fit within a behavioural paradigm, with reinforcement of appropriate behaviour being identified by over 90%' (p. 368).

Of course, behaviourism is not solely about positive reinforcement. Hart refers to ignoring undesired behaviour, but hardly mentions sanctions or punishments. This strikes me as an odd omission in his discussion of approaches to classroom behaviour management. Whilst ignoring unwanted behaviour may seem sensible up to a point, ultimately it is difficult and unwise to continually ignore disruptive behaviour, let alone that which is abusive or dangerous.

No Excuses for Zero Tolerance

The term 'no excuses' became a significant feature of the UK educational discourse following the opening of Michaela Community School – a free school led by Katharine Birbalsingh that proudly embraces a no excuses culture (Kirby, 2016; Porter, 2016). The approach has its antecedents in schools like Mossbourne

Community Academy – where it was established under the headship of Sir Michael Wilshaw, who went on to become HMCI at Ofsted – and it has been embraced by several schools across the UK. However, it is perhaps most closely associated with the charter school model in the USA.

Academic work often suggests that no excuses schools 'promote academic achievement while reinforcing inequality in cultural skills' (Golann, 2015, p. 115) and are grounded in rules which promote whiteness, and position teachers as administrators of compliance and control (Kershen et al., 2019). Meanwhile, the commentators in the press are keen to present no excuses schools as 'workhouses' (George, 2018) and promotors of approaches for which there is no supporting evidence (Murray, 2019). No excuses schools are seen to encourage passivity in students, denying their development of thinking skills. Furthermore, and worse, 'no excuses systems appeared to move many of the teachers to narrow the learning experience to a series of performative tasks to which students had to comply or face harsh punishment' (Kershen et al., 2019, pp. 278-279). In the discourse, 'no excuses' is often associated with 'zero tolerance' – indeed, there do not seem to be demonstrable differences between them – which has been described by the UK's largest teaching union as '"inhumane" and "damaging to pupil mental health"' (Weale, 2019a). Such approaches are criticised as they are thought to 'cause anger, not reflection' (BCU, 2019).

The academic literature which critiques zero-tolerance policies is largely based in the USA, where schools face considerable safeguarding concerns with regard to students bringing in guns and other weapons. Later, the policies were extended to include a zero-tolerance approach to students carrying other prohibited items, such as drugs. Many of the criticisms of zero tolerance within the US context point to the 'school-to-prison pipeline', whilst also highlighting that students of colour are disproportionally punished (Curtis, 2014). Daniels (2009) presents an edited volume of chapters from authors from both sides of the argument, offering an unusually balanced approach to the topic. However, whilst there may be interesting lessons to learn from this literature, it is important to note the significant differences between the US and UK context. Until recently in the USA it was easier for a child to buy a gun than a chocolate egg (Pavey, 2017), and it is not uncommon for schools to employ security guards with metal detectors at the door. As the UK sees a worrying increase in the number of children bringing weapons into school (Coughlan, 2019a), we might understand why schools might wish to take a zero-tolerance approach to the possession of weapons; certainly, as a parent, I think I would probably welcome it.

However, the zero-tolerance discourse often has little to do with weapons. Rather, we might see school websites proclaiming a zero-tolerance approach to bullying, for example. Zero tolerance and no excuses are interchangeable terms, with concerns being raised about responses to, for example, students forgetting pens and so on. The consequences that some schools administer in response to such small infractions have been quite extreme, if one is to believe the anecdotes, with students being placed in isolation for forgetting equipment or for parental failure to pay for school lunches.

Zero-tolerance policies have been linked with isolation booths, which have become an interesting discursive battleground in the fight for the soul of UK schools. Isolation booths are 'barbaric' (Perraudin, 2018), with the Department for Education facing legal action over 'confusing guidance' about how they are to be used (Staufenberg, 2019). The Ban the Booths campaign has garnered widespread support from consultants and politicians, with contributors using #BanTheBooths on Twitter to share horror stories.[2]

The debate around booths was given a boost in January 2020 when the Ban the Booths campaign organised a conference called Lose the Booths. There is an interesting shift in terminology here with 'ban' becoming 'lose', as if there had been a tacit acknowledgement that the imperative verb 'ban' had overtones of authoritarianism that didn't quite gel with the humanistic message that the anti-booth campaigners wanted to convey. But this is a digression. What is most significant is that this event seemed to be a manifestation of a growing concern over schools' use of isolation booths. For instance, the government's children's commissioner,

---

2 See https://banthebooths.co.uk.

Anne Longford, was reported as suggesting that schools 'are converting toilet blocks and classrooms to build isolation booths to accommodate "disruptive" children' (Weale, 2020c), following research conducted by her department. A number of high-profile voices - including politicians - have been calling for tighter regulation of isolation within schools, with suggestions that school leaders should record all instances of isolation, as they are obligated to do with fixed-term and permanent exclusions.

However, much of the discussion seems fuelled by hyperbole and emotive descriptions of children spending months in solitary confinement, with anecdotal horror stories of children with SEND being locked in isolation booths for long periods, and even an apparent suicide attempt taking place in a booth (Perraudin, 2019). In some cases, 'booths' seemed to become associated with solitary confinement.

Lord (2019) gives three examples of people who apparently suffered the torture of isolation booths, leading to complications in later life. The first, Matty, was placed in isolation for reasons that the author thinks some may find 'arbitrary' - reasons such as persistent disruption of lessons, 'bullying', and 'smoking weed' on the school premises. In each of the cases mentioned by Lord, there were significant incidents of misbehaviour. The issue isn't simple - Lord's examples show the complexities involved in behaviour management - but the narrative that booths are being routinely used by schools in ways which contravene human rights needs challenging.

Of course, no one wishes to see children regularly being 'boothed', but it strikes me that the discourse around this topic has been determined by extremes, with any nuance in the discussion being drowned out. Divided spaces such as cubicles - or booths - exist in many environments - for example, libraries, universities and offices. The spaces themselves may provide a useful tool in schools: allowing for undisturbed work or reflection away from potential distractions seems sensible to me. Used as an unrelenting punishment for days or weeks on end would be cruel; happily, I've yet to see any evidence of such usage.

No More Exclusions

The current calls for isolation booths to be banned are matched by calls for school exclusions to be abolished, with Liberal Democrat 2021 London mayoral candidate Siobhan Benita pledging that '"No child in my London will be permanently excluded from main-stream schools"' (Whittaker, 2019). If we are to believe the emotive rhetoric, there is an exclusion crisis in England. However, official figures for England show that in 2017-2018, the rate of permanent exclusions in secondary schools was 0.20%, and for primary schools just 0.03% (Department for Education, 2019d). For fixed-term exclusions, the figures in secondary and primary are 10.13% and 1.40% respectively. Whilst this figure is clearly much higher for secondary schools, it still only amounts to 1,013 students per 10,000 having received a fixed-term exclusion in England during 2017-2018. When this is considered against the misbehaviour experienced by teachers, it seems a remarkably low figure, but as Bennett (2017, p. 17) suggests, there is a 'divergence of perception between senior staff and classroom staff'.

Conversely, the All-Party Parliamentary Group (APPG) on Knife Crime found that 'School exclusions have been increasing at an alarming rate' (N. Smith, 2019, p. 2), citing 'a 70% increase in the number of permanent school exclusions since 2012/13' (p. 3). Despite journalistic reports suggesting otherwise (Schraer, 2019a; Weale, 2019b) the APPG report does highlight 'that a strong corre-lation did not mean that exclusion was directly causing young people to carry knives' (N. Smith, 2019, p. 14), but a 'number of professionals commented that they believed criminal gangs were aware of how school exclusion could increase vulnerability and were seeking to exploit this fact' (p. 14). The APPG report plays an important role in asking the question of what becomes of children who are permanently excluded, recommending that 'All excluded children must have access to the full time education they are legally entitled to - too many do not currently get this' (p. 7).

Restorative Practice

If we are to turn away from no excuses, zero-tolerance behaviour policies and abolish both isolation and exclusion, what alternative might we adopt in order to address misbehaviour in the classroom? One popular option, which is often presented as a more humane approach to behaviour management, is restorative practice. This approach 'originally developed as restorative justice, an approach to crime that focussed on repairing harm and giving a voice to "victims"' (McCluskey et al., 2008, p. 407). Advocates of the approach point to successes in terms of reduced use of isolation and exclusions, with studies suggesting improvements in school culture and student behaviour (e.g. McCluskey et al., 2008; Vaandering, 2014; Short et al., 2018).

Restorative practice is the basis of the approach promoted by Pivotal Education, a behaviour management consultancy founded by Paul Dix, author of the popular book *When the Adults Change, Everything Changes* (2017). In it Dix presents a strong argument for schools to streamline their behaviour management policies and develop simple rules that are articulated by all teachers. He encourages schools to abandon not only severe punishments, but also token reward economies, such as merits. Instead, Dix calls for us to employ calm consistency, praise and 'deliberate botheredness'. He also urges us to ditch improvised responses to misbehaviour, instead making use of 'universal microscripts': 'Most teachers know what they are going to say first when dealing with poor behaviour, but there is rarely a planned middle or a controlled end' (p. 206). He gives an example of such a microscript, designed to empower teachers to deal with difficult situations in a quick, calm and controlled manner, whilst also empowering the student to make better decisions about their behaviour going forward.

Whilst there appears to be great support for restorative practices in schools, the approach is not without its detractors. Early research suggested success in terms of ethos, improved behaviour and teacher views, but more recent work has found that student perceptions are much more negative as teachers seem to be less effective at dealing with poor behaviour (Augustine et al., 2018).

These findings are echoed in concerns voiced by the NASUWT general secretary, Chris Keates, about increases of student misbehaviour in schools that are using restorative practice (Speck, 2019). In one school reported to use the Pivotal approach, staff resorted to strike action due to feeling unsupported by leaders' lack of response to violent students (Chamberlain, 2019). The crucial element here is that teachers must be supported – an element which is explicitly stated by Dix in his explanation of the Pivotal approach in a promotional video dating from 2016: 'Learners are never passed up the hierarchy. We have innovative approaches to ensure teachers at the classroom level remain in charge of the incident but fully supported' (Pivotal Education, 2016) – although this no longer appears on the Pivotal website. As with many approaches to behaviour management, the effectiveness of the Pivotal approach – or of restorative approaches more broadly – lies in their implementation in schools. As Ofsted's Sean Harford warned on Twitter, poorly employed versions of restorative approaches might undermine teachers (Roberts, 2018).

Where restorative practices seem to be most effective is in those schools where a *proactive* form is employed, rather than a merely *reactive* version: 'Proactive practices largely involve integrating restorative techniques into daily school interactions' (Norris, 2019, p. 222). Where school change is driven by solely proactive, or combined proactive and reactive practices, positive impacts are reported. However, in those schools where only reactive restorative practices are employed, the impact seems less effective or less positive (Norris, 2019). This might support the Pivotal approach, in which schools develop a positive culture driven by proactive restorative practices.

Perhaps the schools where there appear to be issues highlight not so much a failure of the approach, but rather the failure of the school to enact it properly, or to stick with it. Certainly, *When the Adults Change, Everything Changes* has received considerable praise from a range of quarters, including classroom teachers. For instance, Holte School in Birmingham reports that 'the use of restorative practice at our school has significantly improved attendance and reduced low-level disruption and exclusions' and that 'Incidents of physical aggression, bullying and discrimination have declined as a result of peer mediation' (Oliver and Farmer, 2019). Holte School is one of many schools that have contributed case studies to the Pivotal website, all of which note similar improvements to behaviour.[3]

One of the issues that emerges in the literature is the necessary involvement of trained specialists in the process. Song and Swearer (2016) note that, in the USA, schools often bring in an outside practitioner to facilitate restorative conversations. It seems a rather obvious thing to say, but teachers are not trained in this kind of work, just as they are not specifically trained in much of the pastoral work they end up doing! But if pastoral leaders wish to develop restorative practice, they may need to provide their staff with more specific, specialist training. Alternatively, should schools be employing counsellors specifically for this kind of work? Perhaps MATs should look to build teams of specialists with specific responsibility for restorative practice, counselling and so on. Perhaps the progressives have identified yet another potential market for neoliberal enterprises!

I see something of an irony in all this. The approaches to behaviour management proposed by Dix are not really a million miles away from those promoted by advocates of no-excuses policies: high expectations, consistency and fairness. Much of the difference seems to be discursive. For instance, whilst 'silent corridors' are demonised by some and cause emotional outrage (BBC News, 2018), Dix (2017, p. 37) celebrates a school that employs 'fantastic walking', meaning every child walking around the school in the same way: 'Every child held the same posture: hands behind their back, chest out, walking tall and proud'. The difference between silent corridors and fantastic walking appears to be that the latter was instigated 'with love, humour and a sense of pride in "our school"' (p. 38). Dix's calls for schools to employ 'deliberate botheredness' strike me as remarkably similar to the language of those schools employing what appears to be an increasingly popular approach to behaviour management called 'warmstrict'.

---

3 See https://pivotaleducation.com/pivotal-case-studies/.

Warmstrict

In their paper about no excuses charter schools, Kershen et al. (2019) seem to point to a discursive trick at play in such school systems where, in an almost Orwellian manipulation of language, *compliance* is dressed up as *care*. Some might argue that this kind of linguistic trickery can be seen echoed in the recent proliferation of a term originating in Lemov (2010): warmstrict.[4] However, as a Twitter hashtag to follow, #warmstrict makes for interesting reading, with students being commended as 'the most improved student this term', schools celebrating various achievement measures and teachers hailing certain approaches - such as greeting students at the door with a smile - as positive examples of warmstrict. The warmstrict mantra could be seen as a modern manifestation of 'tough love', a recognition that behaviour management requires a combination of clear boundaries and nurture. I would suggest that warmstrict therefore aligns with the distinction drawn by Gregory and Cornell (2009) between 'authoritarian' and 'authoritative' approaches to behaviour management. The former refers to zero-tolerance policies, whilst the latter recognises adolescents' need for both structure and support. Gregory and Cornell find that authoritative schools 'were safer and more secure as indicated by lower rates of student victimization by aggression and theft' and 'also had a more welcoming and less hostile peer culture, as perceived by both teachers and students' (p. 110).

What is emphasised in warmstrict is clarity and consistency. The 'strict' element is not about being punitive, and the 'warmth' is driven by a sense of love. Unlike authoritarian approaches, the focus is 'purpose not power' (Lehain, 2019). Lemov (2010) resolves the apparent paradox in warmstrict by highlighting the need to be both warm *and* strict: 'you must be both: caring, funny, warm, concerned, and nurturing—and also strict, by the book, relentless, and sometimes inflexible'. He goes on to say that 'having high expectations is part of caring for and respecting someone' (p. 213).

---

4   Sometimes rendered as warm-strict or, in Lemov's original, Warm/Strict. I have compounded the two elements to form a portmanteau as it appears in the Twitter hashtag.

It could be argued that warmstrict represents a pragmatic synthesis of different approaches to behaviour management, including the different paradigmatic approaches identified by Hart (2010). It encompasses an authoritative (not authoritarian) approach built upon clear boundaries *and* nurture, and one which successfully employs structure *and* support. I would also argue that warmstrict can incorporate the principles of proactive restorative practices in order to foster a positive behaviour culture in schools, where children can feel safe because they know the rules and know that they will be treated with consistency, fairness and kindness. In order to achieve this, the rules and sanctions must be fair and they must also be clearly and regularly articulated so that everyone – students and staff – knows them and understands the consequences of not complying. They must be consistently followed by teachers across the school.

As school leaders, it is important to create whole-school approaches which support teachers with regard to behaviour management. Pragmatic school leaders will consider the range of theoretical and ideological positions set out here, along with any others, and choose approaches which they consider are best suited to supporting teachers and students in their own settings. A pragmatic praxis approach would expect school leaders to continually evaluate and review their policies and procedures to ensure that the best solutions are being employed in the best interests of staff and students.

Practicalities

Having contemplated some broader theoretical and ideological perspectives of behaviour, and having suggested that school leaders should regularly engage in such contemplation, it is important to acknowledge that for most teachers what really matters is what they can do in their own classrooms to create climates which are conducive to learning, and how they should deal with disruptive, rude or aggressive behaviour.

In Chapter 4 we discussed Nassem's (2019) important identification of the institutional bullying which can occur in schools - with teachers ignoring or even encouraging bullying - and we reflected briefly on the correlation between language and thought, noting that the language that we use to talk about something can affect the ways in which we think about it, and vice versa.

In her popular book *Getting the Buggers to Behave* (2010), Cowley happily dismisses theory, promising readers that the book will provide practical tips and advice. True to her word, she outlines practical steps that teachers can take to establish positive behaviour in the classroom. In fairness, despite the lack of theoretical positioning, Cowley presents some sound, common-sense suggestions which are grounded in the daily realities of the classroom, and I would certainly be happy to recommend that teachers take a look at it. Whilst it is probably especially pertinent to those teachers at the beginning of their career, there would certainly be no harm in established teachers taking time to peruse its pages as part of their developing pragmatic approach to praxis.

One name which cannot be ignored in discussions about behaviour management is Bill Rogers, who has written several titles on the topic, and from whom there is a wealth of instructional videos available on YouTube. Probably the best place to start is his seminal title *You Know the Fair Rule*; first published in 1997, the book is now in its third edition (2011). Whilst Cowley explicitly disavows theory, Rogers acknowledges the theoretical positioning of his approach to behaviour management in the endnote to the preface, but does not burden the text with multitudinous academic references. Thus, the book is easy to read but full of informed suggestions, providing a model of pragmatic praxis.

Rogers talks not of 'behaviour management', preferring 'discipline', almost reclaiming a term that has fallen out of fashion. He outlines in the first chapter his three uses of the term: preventative discipline, corrective discipline and supportive discipline. He then goes on to give specific techniques which, just as Cowley does, he illustrates with vignettes and scenarios. This affords a useful practicability to the approach. What clearly stands out in this work is the importance of calm, rational responses to misbehaviour. One of the things that Rogers is keen to point out is the importance of focusing on primary behaviour and ignoring secondary behaviour. For instance, imagine that a student has interrupted a teacher's exposition by speaking to a peer across the classroom. As the teacher challenges this behaviour, the student sighs and rolls their eyes. What should the teacher now do? In many cases, we might find ourselves being irritated by what we perceive as a slight, raising our voice and demanding, 'Don't you roll your eyes at me!' This kind of escalation detracts from the initial misbehaviour and potentially generates an unresolvable problem, resulting in escalating levels of threat and punishment. Responding to secondary behaviour, and thus exacerbating the situation, is something that I know I have been guilty of and have often seen other teachers do.

Another key suggestion offered by Rogers is to develop a 'discipline plan'. A similar suggestion appears in Dix (2017) in the form of microscripts, but for Rogers (2011, p. 50) the idea is more akin to a lesson plan, encouraging teachers to think in advance about their responses to disruption by asking fundamental questions about how they might respond to behaviour incidents.

I once worked in a school that had the reputation of being the worst in town, and the town had the reputation for having the worst schools in the county. Behaviour there was certainly challenging. I recall whole-staff training on the notion of developing a behaviour plan to think through what our expectations were and how we would respond to particular issues. This was the first time (and, in fact, the last) that such a thing had been suggested to me, despite having been a qualified teacher for some years at that stage. It seems obvious now. But when I mention the idea of a behaviour plan to colleagues and students on ITT placements, it seems like a revelation to them.

Having taught a little bit of Key Stage 3 computer science, I find that computational thinking offers a useful language for thinking about and developing a discipline plan using an IF/THEN/ELSE model. This is also applicable to lesson plans. IF the class know X, THEN teach Y. ELSE reteach X. In behaviour management, this could be extended to consider the range of potential misbehaviours we are likely to encounter. Whilst I am resistant to any attempts to reduce teaching down to a set of algorithms, thinking about behaviour management as a flowchart is helpful. It equips teachers with a set of pre-thought-out tools that help to avoid frustration and undue escalation of issues. It helps to keep us calm. Computational thinking also leads us onto discipline via choices and consequences. When a student is displaying inappropriate or disruptive behaviour, it is sensible to calmly present choices to them – IF the student continues with behaviour X, THEN …, ELSE … – restating the behaviour that you want in calm, polite and positive language (see Rogers (2011) for excellent examples of language for behaviour leadership).

In addition to the writers and resources mentioned here, I asked Twitter for other suggestions.[5] Names that came up in replies included Roland Chaplain, John Visser, Robert and Jana Marzano, Lee Canter, Jackie Ward, Jarlath O'Brien, Jason Bangbala and Michael Ryan Hunsaker. From the various suggestions made, one text in particular stands out: Louise Porter's *Behaviour in Schools* (2014), which, as its subtitle suggests, promises 'theory and practice for teachers'.

Conclusion

Effective behaviour management is the consequence of positive school cultures (Bennett, 2017), and school leaders should be thinking clearly about what they want their school culture to be. It's far too easy to wind up with laminated lists of rules stuck to every classroom wall that ultimately get ignored because children have tested the boundaries and found them full of weaknesses. School behaviour cultures should be built upon the premise of high regard for all, with a strong sense of high expectations born of love. But there needs to be clear and consistent consequences for misbehaviour, whether schools utilise a restorative approach or not. Students need to see that poor behaviour is not to be accepted, teachers need to feel supported by their leaders so they can feel confident to teach their lessons, and students need to be allowed to learn.

---

5 Twitter, 17 February 2020. Available at: https://twitter.com/sputniksteve/status/1229448945060978688?s=20.

Amidst the noise about zero tolerance, no excuses, isolation booths, exclusions, restorative practice and so on, it is important to keep our in-school messages clear. Have clear and simple rules that can become easily articulated, non-negotiable expectations. As classroom teachers, develop discipline plans that enable you to respond to misbehaviour and disruption in a calm, considered and consistent fashion.

I would like to point out here that in England and Wales the criminal age of responsibility is 10 years old. With the severity of consequence that comes from that, I think we are doing a massive disservice to our young people if we do not employ sanctions within the school setting. It is imperative that children and teenagers learn to be responsible for their actions, even if this does not sit well with their biological development. No amount of restorative conversation is going to keep a teenager out of prison for committing a serious crime. However, children who misbehave are still children, and teachers who respond poorly are still people. Alongside whatever sanctions we employ, it is important that incidents of misbehaviour are treated with compassion for all involved. Poor behaviour has serious implications for everyone. Even 'low-level' disruption can significantly impact upon social relations between students and between children and adults.

Most importantly, whatever discipline strategies you employ in your classroom - or policies you adopt as a school leader - it is imperative that they are grounded in careful and deliberate thinking. The pragmatic practitioner must be able to explain why they are doing what they are doing.

My key recommendations include:

- Build a strong and positive culture through high expectations and fair and consistent sanctions.
- Remain calm when faced with poor behaviour by making consistent use of the school behaviour policy. If you are a leader, equip teachers with clear procedures that can be applied consistently across the board.

- Use incidents of poor behaviour as teachable moments. Issue sanctions, but discuss with students the issues and consequences arising from the behaviour choices they make.

- Read widely around the subject of behaviour management in order to develop considered, thoughtful approaches and policies.

Chapter 7

Character

Introduction

The 2019 revised Ofsted inspection framework makes judgements against four key areas: quality of education, behaviour and attitudes, personal development, and leadership and management. It is interesting that personal development gets a judgement all of its own, within which we are told that Ofsted (2019b, p. 11) want to see that 'the curriculum and the provider's wider work support learners to develop their character – including their resilience, confidence and independence – and help them know how to keep physically and mentally healthy'.

The prominence of character education in the Ofsted framework comes as no surprise: I was co-organiser of #CharacterED2018 – a conference on the theme of character education held at Lichfield Cathedral School on 12 May 2018 – at which Sean Harford spoke about the place of character education within Ofsted thinking and former secretary of state for education Nicky Morgan spoke of her belief in the importance of character education as part of the school curriculum. The following year, Damian Hinds, the then secretary of state for education, signalled the growing focus on character at the Department for Education and Ofsted (Department for Education and Hinds, 2019b). The Department for Education (2019b) then released its framework guidance on character education later that year.

Character education is, like most of education, a contentious topic. This is perfectly illustrated by the debate held by the Policy Exchange in 2014 in which speakers debated the motion 'Teaching character education in schools is a waste of time'. In this debate, and in a follow-up article for *The Spectator*, Toby Young (2014) argued that curriculum time should not be devoted to character education because 'character traits are inherited, not taught'. This is an argument that can be challenged, as Baehr (2017, p. 1157) points out: 'There is at least some evidence for thinking that elementary and secondary schools can have a favorable impact on the moral and civic character of their students'.

Equally, Arthur and O'Shaugnessy (2012, p. 2) state that 'The research literature shows a clear and positive correlation between character education and academic attainment'. They provide a brief summary of examples of this literature, pointing to clear positive impacts upon academic attainment of identified character traits. However, I can't help but feel a little saddened that character education is seen of value only in the context of its impact upon academic outcomes.

Young (2014) reasserts the position that *knowledge* must be the foundation of the curriculum, as opposed to those soft skills such as resilience and so on. He cites Hirsch in this call, but even Hirsch recognises the importance of character education: 'Classic texts on education such as Plato's *Republic* and Locke's *Some Thoughts Concerning Education* emphasize that character development and virtue are far more important educational goals than mere acquisition of knowledge' (Hirsch, 2013). Hirsch, in fact, sees that knowledge is of foundational importance in the development of character, a position which is not quite aligned with Young's argument of the immovable inheritability of character. That knowledge might be the foundation of character is a suggestion not unlike the notion of phronesis – practical wisdom or practical virtue. We might conceive of this as a practical, real-world application of the knowledge that we have been taught and gained through experiences. It is the idea of a deliberate set of actions informed by deliberate thinking – essentially, it is praxis. Here we might see how praxis is an ideal pursuit to develop in children and young people: a goal or ambition as worthy as anything that the materialistic, instrumentalist world of work and consumerism has to offer us.

So, the essential question in the debate around character education is not whether or not it *can* be taught, but whether or not it *should* be taught. It is my contention that character both can and ought to be taught as part of an unhidden, knowledge-rich pastoral curriculum. Otherwise, we leave character development to the hidden curriculum of the playground, the changing room, social media and the world beyond the school walls.

Defining Character Education

In his 2019 speech to the Church of England Foundation for Educational Leadership conference, the then secretary of state for education Damien Hinds outlined 'five foundations for building character' (Department for Education and Hinds, 2019b). At first, I was a little sceptical. The foundations he gave were sport, creativity, performing, volunteering and membership, and the world of work. Now, I have no problem with these strands per se – each has value in its own right, and I can see how they link to the qualities mentioned in the Ofsted framework. However, at the time this struck me as something of a missed opportunity, or of offering schools a rather easy way of hitting Ofsted requirements. Perhaps the foundations seemed to represent a rather old-fashioned view of character – that character formation is achieved through competitive sports and being involved in school shows: that such things help you to build resilience and teamwork. The fifth category, the world of work, is always a concern for me because I don't want schools to be positioned as centres of job training.

However, Hinds outlines the urgency of the need for character education to address issues around resilience, mental health and wellbeing in the age of social media, which makes young people vulnerable to 'the adverse, artificial impression of curated and altered images, the kind of visual enhancement which depicts people with perfect lives and perfect bodies' (Department for Education and Hinds, 2019b). He talks about 'resilience', quoting a 10-year-old with whom he had spoken who defined resilience as: '"It's just believing in yourself, really, isn't it?"' For Lucas and Spencer, 'resilience' is one aspect of what they call 'tenacity', which they closely associate with character (Lucas and Spencer, 2018).

Whilst reasons they give for the importance of tenacity include 'satisfaction to learners' and its value 'across societies and cultures' (p. 33), they also do a good job of grounding the need for tenacity within what I would describe as a utilitarian or consequentialist conceptualisation of educational purpose, in which students need skills for a particular set of identified or identifiable circumstances. Most notably, under 'what it is to be employable', they cite the Confederation of British Industry (CBI), which they say has been 'explicit about the need for schools to develop determined, resilient tenacious potential employees' (p. 35). Whilst there may be an argument for the need to encourage grit, resilience and tenacity in students, the last place we should be looking to inform school policy is the CBI! To view students as 'potential employees' is deeply troubling for me. However, with that minor gripe aside, Lucas and Spencer outline a range of strategies for developing what they call 'tenacity' alongside domain-specific knowledge and skills, and there's much there that I would recommend, at least for consideration, as with the companion title *Teaching Creative Thinking* (Lucas and Spencer, 2017). Whilst not explicitly about character education, the traits that are explored under the banner of creativity closely align with those associated with character and, whilst I might have some fundamental disagreements with Lucas and Spencer over some of the pedagogical claims they make, I would urge pragmatic practitioners to consider the advice in these texts.

Doing Character Education

The Jubilee Centre has been doing some interesting work around character education and has developed a useful model of the 'building blocks of character' (Jubilee Centre for Character and Virtues, 2017, p. 5). The model presents four virtues - intellectual, moral, civic and performance - which lead to 'practical wisdom' (p. 5). Examples are presented under each heading: autonomy, curiosity and judgement are intellectual virtues; compassion, humility and integrity are moral virtues; and so on.

I must confess to having been a little apprehensive about some of these traits; they risk the trap of being nothing more than nebulous generic skills, which we know lack the stickability of domain-specific knowledge. The answer to this, I think, is to turn them into domain-specific artefacts. One way to do this is to apply the traits as descriptors, and to think about examples of where we might have seen them.

For example, my colleague Jo Owens[1] had the idea of using the Jubilee Centre's framework in our English lessons to create a display about the character of Atticus Finch in *To Kill a Mockingbird*. We did this with our Year 9 classes, having them think of moments in the novel when Finch demonstrates these skills and provide quotations. This gave us some really nice 'Englishy' work on Harper Lee's presentation of the character, but it also provided us with proof of concept for the application of these trait descriptors in discussions about what makes a moral character. With my class, I discussed the obvious fact that Finch is a fictional character - an archetype and a different kind of protagonist to, say, the comic book heroes which dominate the current box office smashes of DC and Marvel. We also did some critical work on the representation of black people in the novel and the notion of Finch as a white saviour.

More recently, I have applied the same idea to R. C. Sherriff's *Journey's End,* identifying points in the play when various characters display traits such as compassion, courage and humility. But in this instance, we thought about the flaws that the characters might show which either inhibit their ability to demonstrate a given positive trait or demonstrate its opposite. So, we might think of antonyms for some of the words in the Jubilee Centre's framework, such as indifference, cowardice and arrogance. This enables a discussion around how actions might be perceived differently - is Hibbert's claim of neuralgia born of cowardice, as Stanhope insists, or from fear? Does Stanhope's ultimate treatment of Hibbert demonstrate compassion, and even humility?

These kinds of discussions equip students with the language they need in order to discuss characters in English literature, but this could easily be developed into wider personal development discussions in, for example, PSHE education. The terms could be used in the abstract to discuss hypothetical situations involving fictional children involved in difficult peer relationships, for example. Or, perhaps, a class could discuss the kinds of situations in which an individual might be able to demonstrate the various traits. It might even be tempting to engage students in discussions or other

---

1   Find her @joanneowens on Twitter.

activities in which they are prompted to reflect more obviously upon their own experiences, perhaps recording moments when they have shown the traits themselves.

So, the virtues of the Jubilee Centre model present a useful framework for literary analysis – exploring the presentation of fictional characters – but also a framework for discussing personal development. There have been many occasions over my years in teaching when I have been asked to help students to write personal statements for UCAS or, indeed, job applications. As a middle leader, I have read applications for teaching vacancies. It has become quite clear to me that people generally find this kind of writing incredibly difficult, and it often ends up being very formulaic. However, if we could encourage students to reflect on their own actions in relation to the model of virtues, this might enable them to better construct the kinds of self-narratives that would be beneficial to these applications. Using the language of these virtues, and giving examples of when we have demonstrated them, enables us to think about our qualities beyond the narrowly academic realm of examination results, or the outcomes of competitive activities such as sports. Furthermore, having such a framework enables us to identify those behaviours which we might wish to nurture and cultivate in ourselves and those we teach.

Via its website, the Jubilee Centre offers a wide range of resources for teachers and parents around character education.[2] Amongst the resources for teachers are lesson plans for all key stages that enable the teaching of character and virtues through subjects, or as a discrete subject of its own. These resources are well worth perusing. In addition to curriculum and lesson materials, the Jubilee Centre website holds a library of academic materials, amongst which you will find strong arguments supporting character education.

Several schools have embraced the character education movement, and it is not hard to find examples with their own programmes. The University of Birmingham School has, unsurprisingly, embedded the Jubilee Centre's work within its ethos. On the school website, the principal Colin Townsend says: 'Our core purpose is to

2 See https://www.jubileecentre.ac.uk.

develop the character of our children – their personal qualities, or virtues – so they can go on and become happy, engaged, fulfilled citizens.'[3] This free school demonstrates its commitment to character education through its personal learning and development curriculum, and infuses the taught academic curriculum with character. In nearby Staffordshire, schools in the John Taylor MAT have embedded character education through their STRIPE curriculum, which aims to build the following skills/dispositions: self-manager, team player, reflective and resilient, innovate and create, participator, enquirer. According to the John Taylor Free School website, 'unlike some "blended" learning/topic-based study, STRIPE achieves [a range of outcomes] without compromising the academic and assessment rigour of a traditional subject-by-subject offer'.[4]

One of the questions around character education regards the extent to which we might be able to assess it – and whether we should even try. The Jubilee Centre's resources include performative criteria written in child-friendly 'I can …' type statements. Using these to drive self-assessment might enable students to reflect critically upon their own behaviours and conduct, and equip them with a language to discuss character traits in a more analytical fashion.

In 2017, the National Foundation for Educational Research (NFER) published a report featuring five case studies of schools' character education programmes (Walker et al., 2017). The examples include primary and secondary schools, each adopting quite different approaches but with common strands. The report concludes by drawing out 'five key features of the effective leadership of character education' (p. 40). These are:

1. Senior leaders must drive it and all teachers must deliver it.

2. Place at the core of the school ethos.

3. Take a long-term approach.

---

3 See https://uobschool.org.uk.
4 See https://www.johntaylorfreeschool.co.uk/the-curriculum.

4. Build a collective understanding and language.

5. Maintain focus, momentum and ongoing communication.

(Walker et al., 2017, pp. 40–41)

As noted previously, however, character education is not without its critics. As Kristjánsson (2013, p. 269) highlights, 'The aim of cultivating (moral) character and virtue through virtue education in schools continues to be described as controversial'; but he describes the controversy as 'baffling'.

Whilst Kristjánsson mounts a credible defence of character education against various concerns, Sanderse (2019) launches a further attack on both character education and the concept of *Bildung*, between which he sees parallels. He sees both as having lost their potency through being co-opted by governments to serve problematic or nefarious agendas. For instance, he sees character education as being defined in instrumentalist terms: 'virtues are not seen as constitutive of a happy life, but as means to become successful in school or in the job market' (p. 408). He also suggests that character education programmes reflect neoliberal movements and that the 'revolutionary potential' of *Bildung* gave way to 'to growing conservatism and nationalism' (p. 410). For Sanderse, both *Bildung* and character education can be 'characterised by a nationalistic and utilitarian way of thinking' (p. 410). However, I lean towards Kristjánsson's more optimistic perspective, albeit with his caveat that 'well-founded misgivings about virtue education do remain' (2013, p. 285). Teachers and school leaders seeking to introduce or develop character education should therefore adopt the informed pragmatic approach of reading widely around the subject and weighing up the various arguments.

But, inevitably, the question must arise of why we need character education at all.

Looking for Rubies

There is a strong vein in the educational discourse about the perceived negative impact upon students of what might be called performative, neoliberal education systems. This is seen at university level (e.g. Ball, 2015) and in schools (e.g. Trotman, 2016). Claxton and Lucas (2015, 2016) identify a school system which inculcates a narrow focus on exam grades and accountability measures, and give a number of personal accounts from children and parents for whom this focus results in feelings of poor self-worth and high levels of stress. In addition, they suggest that the current schooling system, focused as it is on exam results, leaves young people with insufficient resilience and fewer coping strategies than they will need in adult life.

Claxton and Lucas (2015) introduce us to Ruby. Initially presented in the guise of a thought experiment, Ruby becomes a vehicle for exploration of what we might mean by a 'great education', as Ruby claims to have received, despite mediocre exam results. Ruby's explanation details the 'seven Cs' – confidence, collaboration, communication, creativity, curiosity, commitment and craftsmanship – which become features of what Claxton and Lucas call 'character'. In contrast, via Ruby's friend Nadezna, who attended a school nearby, they present a list of negative traits which they dub the 'seven Ds': defeated, disengaged, distanced, dumb, deadbeat, drifter and dogsbody. A further contrast is presented in the figure of Eric who, despite academic success at school, has grown into an adult suffering from imposter syndrome and in need of counselling. It transpires that Ruby, Nadezna and Eric are fictions, in the mould of Rousseau's *Emile* (1979 [1762]), but through them Claxton and Lucas explore what else beyond exam content students might be learning in school.

Claxton and Lucas go on to outline some suggestions for what a character development curriculum might include, examples of what they see as good practice in a range of schools, and advice for parents. Throughout the book, the authors make several references to what young people will need in work, claiming, for example, that Google won't employ people who know their own IQ scores. Whilst this is a claim that I have no inclination to investigate or verify, it does point to a problematic tendency in some quarters to position schooling as a kind of job training. Ironically, this often comes alongside criticisms of schooling as following a factory model, producing automatons for employment in low-intellect, low-wage manual labour. Now we should be teaching children to be creative so that they can … work for Google or Apple.

At one point in their book, Claxton and Lucas suggest that schooling is made worse by irrelevance. For instance, they assert: 'It is a rare parent (or teacher) who is able to come up with a convincing reason why every 15-year-old needs to know the difference between metamorphic and igneous rocks or to explain the subplots in *Othello*' (2015, pp. 7–8). I would simply suggest here that, just as it problematic to tell them they need it 'for the exam', it is equally troublesome to posit that curriculum should be made 'relevant' to, and crafted around, an idea about the future world of work. Indeed, if we were to strip the curriculum of everything that most people won't need for their job, then there wouldn't be very much left. This isn't what schooling is about as far as I'm concerned (for more on my concerns, see Lane, 2016). This aside, the book does pose relevant and important questions about what school should be for, the damage that schooling might cause and the role that character education might play in addressing some of these concerns.

Watch and Punish

In Chapter 6 we considered different ideas about, and approaches towards, behaviour management. Inevitably, there is a dynamic relationship between behaviour and character – a 'good' character can be defined as exhibiting those behaviours that we would wish our fellow citizens to display. It could be argued that schools' attempts to 'improve' behaviour are an ongoing experiment in character formation: moulding and shaping our students into the 'best versions of themselves', where what that really means is 'versions of themselves that best conform to societal expectations'. Certainly, many critical-theory-based analyses of schooling take this approach, often pointing to work like Illich's *Deschooling Society* (1971) and suggesting that schooling removes from children their ability to be creative, imaginative or inquisitive. In this kind of analysis, children are shaped to be nothing more than mindless automatons, ready to follow orders and not much else.

Biesta (2016) suggests that schools are particularly good at qualification and socialisation, but not so good at what he calls subjectification. In other words, schools are very good at measurement and examination – and they are very good at teaching children how to behave – but weak at subjectification, which 'has to do with emancipation and freedom and with the responsibility that comes with such freedom' (p. 4). Here, Biesta is referring to the philosophical concept of the *subject*, which is an incredibly complex concept with a long history (Rebughini, 2014). As a gross simplification, we can conceive of the subject as an individual with agency. I would argue that character education is incredibly well placed to inculcate in students a sense of the responsibility that comes with the freedom of being individual subjects with their own agency.

One of the methods that schools often employ to encourage students to improve their behaviour is the report card. It might not be called this, of course: schools use euphemisms to ameliorate any negative connotations. So maybe it is called an Attitude to Learning (ATL) Monitoring Card. Or maybe it is a Success Card. Perhaps it's a Star Rating Card. Or it might be a Rainbow of Delight Card. Or a Metaphor of Acceptability Card. Whatever. And usually it's not a card, it's a booklet – a week's worth of empty spaces, five per day or one for however many lessons the school operates. The principle is simple: the student presents their report card to the teacher at the start of each lesson; the teacher records a score and perhaps a comment on how well behaved or attentive the student has been; and the student shows this report to their form tutor or head of year once a day or once a week. There might be a minimum expected score and any time the student gains below that they are issued with a sanction. Anything higher might result in merits, house points or some other token of praise. Often, the student's behaviour will improve for a while in lessons, but perhaps not at other times in the school day. And perhaps the improvement is not sustained once they are no longer on report. This sort of device does not in itself produce the long-term effects that we might hope for because it does not instil in the student the ways of being that are conducive to success – either academically or socially. One student told me that he felt the report worked for him in lessons because he knew that he was being watched, but that this did not apply outside of lessons. I suggested that he could imagine a drone following him everywhere to film him, allowing us to see everything.

In *Discipline and Punish*, Foucault describes Jeremy Bentham's design for a prison called a panopticon. The design is simple yet wonderful: a circular building with cells arranged around a central observation tower. From the tower, the guards can peer into any of the cells; from the cells, it is impossible for the prisoners to know if they are being observed or not. 'Hence the major effect of the Panopticon: to induce in the inmate a state of conscious and per-manent visibility that assures the automatic functioning of power' (Foucault, 1991, p. 201). The design of the panopticon need not be limited in use to prisons, but can be applied to any institution – such as hospitals or schools – where surveillance might be desired.

It is in *Discipline and Punish* that we find one of Foucault's most well-known observations, the oft-quoted 'Is it surprising that pris-ons resemble factories, schools, barracks, hospitals, which all resemble prisons?' (p. 228). This is usually taken to imply some-thing sinister about schools – that children are inmates who have been caged like the rhetorical bird of William Blake's 'The Schoolboy'. But it is a mistake, I think, to see in Foucault's work a purely pejorative description; rather, he presents the panopticon as a transformative moment in the development of a surveillance culture in which power is productive rather than solely oppressive. Elsewhere, Foucault (1980, p. 147) notes that Bentham designed the panopticon following an idea from his brother, who had visited a military training school. What both Bentham and Foucault seek to promote is the notion of visibility or transparency (Brunon-Ernst, 2016). For Bentham, this transparency is just as applicable to those in positions of authority as it is to those in positions of incarceration:

In this sense, the people always retain the right to deny public functionaries the exercise of sovereignty. The people can take back the
power they have given, and in that sense public functionaries possess
only a fiduciary power. If they do not make proper use of the power
they have been entrusted with, they are immediately divested of that
power.

(Brunon-Ernst, 2016, p. 148).

It is interesting to note that the original French title of Foucault's
Discipline and Punish is *Surveiller et punir*, meaning to watch and
punish, or as Google Translate suggests, 'to keep an eye on and
punish'. So this notion of watching, or keeping an eye on, is central
to Foucault's exposition of the effect of the panopticon and his
theory of panopticism, which he presents as a positive development in a liberal society. To Foucault, 'the Panopticon is characteristic
of a liberal government, where freedom should be protected and
fabricated by the means of political and judicial checks as well as
procedures of control' (Leroy, 2016, p. 143). But more than this, the
idealised conceptualisation of a surveillance society is not necessarily about the eternal gaze of some outside force. Rather, it is
about an internalised sense of surveillance, an internalised permanent gaze (Foucault, 1980).

Of course, it is possible to see in Foucault's writing a sense of the
prophetic - that we now live in an age of surveillance through
CCTV and governmental snooping on our online activities. The
apparent shock caused by revelations of Cambridge Analytica's
trawling of data and targeted political advertising during both the
2016 US presidential election campaign and the 2016 referendum
on the UK's membership of the EU suggested that we are naive to
the amount of data that we produce. There is an argument that this
kind of surveillance is not the same as that envisaged by Bentham
and Foucault, since we do not know that we are being watched
(McMullan, 2015). However, I would argue that we shouldn't be
surprised by any of these recent developments: we all know about
CCTV and we all choose to ignore the terms and conditions
offered up to us by the various digital devices which we own and
the various contracts which we voluntarily sign. This vision of the
surveillance culture in which we live has often been likened to that

described by George Orwell in *1984*, with Big Brother taking the form of various instruments of surveillance. Ironically, the popular 'reality' TV show which takes its name from Orwell inverts the notion: in *Big Brother*, it is the audience - us - who is doing the surveillance. But I digress.

Foucault, like Bentham before him, sees in this surveillance society a positive outcome: a liberal society in which the freedom of citizens is ensured through an internalised gaze. Working in a Christian school context, the notion of an eternal gaze is inevitably aided by a conceptualised omnipotent other - God. I don't propose in this little book to explore theology, or the criticisms aimed at religious belief; feel free to read Dawkins and the other high priests of the new atheism. I will simply posit here that for our current purposes 'God' can be a handy personification of the eternal gaze that Bentham and Foucault explore. And promises of eternal life aren't really what it's all about; rather, if we were to actually follow the Golden Rule, or Jesus' second commandment, then the Kingdom of God would be made a reality - a community of people being nice to each other.

We want our students to conduct themselves not only to be obedient, but to do the *right thing*. I'm reminded of the maxim (often misattributed to C. S. Lewis) which teaches us that integrity is doing the right thing even when no one is watching. However, I'm not entirely convinced that this is correct. What I think Bentham and Foucault are inevitably alluding to is a sense of conscience - the inner voice that guides our moral judgements. Ultimately, we cannot ever escape our own gaze; the Self is the inevitable judge of its own actions. Whether one conceives of this as an internalised panopticon, as Big Brother or as the eternal gaze of God is irrelevant. What matters is conduct.

Conclusion

As a sign of the increasing interest in character education, in the summer of 2019 the Department for Education (2019a) launched a call for evidence on character and resilience. It also teamed up with the Jubilee Centre for Character and Virtues (2019) to relaunch the National Character Awards. Furthermore, a forthcoming special edition of the Chartered College of Teaching's journal *Impact* will focus on youth social action and character education.

Whilst these developments are potentially quite exciting, I do fear that the conceptualisation of character education which is emerging is too centred on those 'soft skills' such as resilience and grit which ultimately mean nothing and get us nowhere. I find myself in many ways agreeing with Robinson's critique of this conceptualisation. His observation that the Old English term *caracter* referred to a 'symbol marked on the body or an imprint on the soul' (Robinson, 2014) is a powerful sentiment: character is an imprint on the soul. Robinson also talks of character in the dramatic sense, referring to Brecht's corridor of choices, suggesting that 'Character is partly how we respond to choices'.

For me, this should be the essence of character education. It should be the deliberate, unhidden teaching of those traits which we believe are beneficial to the children in our care, and to the society to which they belong. It is to nurture those traits that we believe will lead to human flourishing. It is the imbibing of those traits which we wish to become the habits of a good life.

Some suggestions to help do this might include:

▦ Develop a clear working definition of 'character' and of the traits that you wish to inculcate in your students.

▦ Include these traits in the golden threads of your knowledge-rich pastoral curriculum.

▦ Seek opportunities to discuss these traits across subject domains.

▦ Reaffirm these traits at every opportunity, and particularly when you can explore them at length - for example, in assemblies.

- Acknowledge when students demonstrate these traits.
- Perhaps most importantly, demonstrate these traits yourself.

Chapter 8

Remote Pastoral

Introduction

In 2020 the entire world was shaken by an unprecedented pandemic which saw schools in many countries close their gates to all but the children of key workers.[1] Across the UK, teachers suddenly found themselves having to engage with remote and distance learning. For some, this was no huge leap, having been using various technologies to produce materials and interact with their students beyond the classroom as a matter of course. For others, this was a steep learning curve as they grappled with unfamiliar technologies, delivering content and providing assessment in new ways. A lot of individuals, schools and organisations generously made materials available for free or at reduced cost. Sir Patrick Stewart delivered a daily Shakespeare sonnet on Instagram. There was a lot of content.

As the closure of UK schools was announced, immediate concern arose about SATs, GCSE and A level exams. There were understandable questions about how students would be awarded fair grades that were an accurate reflection of their knowledge and effort. There was also concern about the welfare of students in Years 11 and 13 as they were forced to come to terms with their mixed feelings about this sudden departure from education and qualification as we know it.

But whilst the press and mainstream media were focused on the technicalities of fair grading following the lockdown, many practitioners were expressing worries about students' wellbeing more generally. How can schools address the pastoral needs of our vulnerable children and young people? How can we ensure that

---

1 I say 'was' with the hopeful optimism that by the time you are reading this it might all be over, but as this book is being written and edited (June 2020), we are very much still in the middle of it. The ease out of lockdown and the reopening of schools is just beginning.

children in troubled homes are safe? How can we check on those who are known to self-harm?

It soon emerged that many teachers and schools were continuing to take their pastoral obligations seriously, with regular home contact by telephone, email and – in some cases – visits. Much of this contact has been targeted at students who are known to be vulnerable, although some schools have been keeping regular contact with all their students. However, there are many children whose vulnerabilities are unknown to teachers or any other adults outside of the home – or perhaps even to those within the home. Some children, whilst they may not show any obvious signs, may nonetheless be experiencing trauma or distress. For them, school is a safe haven: that daily contact with friends, teachers and other members of the community is an important interaction with a support network that was suddenly taken away from them.

For all children, the imposed lockdown measures meant that they found themselves in strange and potentially troubling circumstances. I consider myself fortunate – we have a nice family home with a good-sized garden in which our children are able to run around and we are all able to get that all-important bit of fresh air. For families living in accommodation without access to private outdoor space, being asked to stay home may feel like confinement. Even those of us with such space are likely to have experienced a sense of cabin fever. The lack of contact with friends and relatives during lockdown could have profoundly negative impacts on the mental health and wellbeing of a large number of people, not least children and adolescents.

Schools have engaged in the rapid adoption of remote learning strategies and technologies to enable home working, including the adaptation and updating of safeguarding policies and communication protocols in order to provide students with the best learning experiences possible. But more than this, schools have been at the forefront of supporting identified vulnerable children and the children of key workers. Despite the challenges in maintaining social distancing, schools have remained open for these children. Some schools have been providing a lifeline of food and other resources to families in need.

Homeschooling

Of course, none of this is particularly new. Many schools, and most universities, have been operating these kinds of systems for some time. Online learning platforms and massive open online courses (MOOCs) have been a staple of much provision. Most famously, perhaps, the Open University has been operating along these principles since its establishment in 1969. Homeschooling is nothing new, and the modern homeschooling movement has been growing since the 1970s and John Holt's advocacy of 'unschooling'.[2] A range of claims are made about the efficacy of homeschooling, including with regard to academic attainment, civil engagement and happiness, although such claims are not supported empirically (Lubienski et al., 2013).

In the UK, parents are allowed to remove their children from school but are obliged to give them an equivalent full-time education. Local councils are permitted to make an 'informal enquiry' to ensure that this is being provided, and can serve a School Attendance Order if they think the child needs to be taught at school.[3] Whilst there does not seem to be as strong a unified movement in the UK as there is in the USA, homeschooling in the UK is growing (Issimdar, 2018), with support groups, various organisations and commercial companies providing a range of resources, materials and courses.

However, the unregulated nature of homeschooling has led to safeguarding concerns being raised about 'illegal schools' (Humanists UK, 2019) and vulnerable children who may fall off the radar (Ofsted and Schooling, 2017), leading to a governmental consultation on plans to establish a register of children who are not attending mainstream school.[4]

Despite these concerns, and although there are clearly moves to increase regulation, I have struggled to find explicit guidance about pastoral support for children who are being homeschooled.

2 See https://responsiblehomeschooling.org/homeschooling-101/a-brief-history-of-homeschooling/; and https://www.britannica.com/topic/homeschooling.
3 See https://www.gov.uk/home-education.
4 See https://www.gov.uk/government/consultations/children-not-in-school.

I have no doubt that most parents who choose to homeschool their children will want to provide a robust and comprehensive curriculum that includes aspects of the pastoral as suggested in Chapter 3, and to develop a sense of character as explored in Chapter 7. However, for children who are perhaps not blessed with such family support, being out of school could be problematic. As noted in Chapter 6, the discussions around behaviour management include serious concerns about the potential adverse effects of exclusion from school; such effects are likely to be amplified during any extended period of school closure. The concerns noted about illegal schools also include reports that some children have been denied what might be considered foundational knowledge due to extreme conservative or orthodox religious beliefs. In such circumstances, we might find that children's personal development has been negatively impacted, and that they may be prone to extremist doctrines.

Conclusion

In the immediate aftermath of school closures as a result of the COVID-19 crisis, schools' collective first concern was, understandably, to ensure the provision of teaching and learning through various technologies and media. Pastoral leaders, however, have rightly turned their attention to the ongoing pastoral needs and wellbeing of their students, considering strategies for maintaining contact beyond simply setting and assessing work.

There has been much talk across social and traditional media about the long-term impact of COVID-19: will society be drastically altered? For schools, there may well be profound questions to ask and radical answers to provide. My guess is that we will inevitably return to convention, but the questions that we ask ourselves as we navigate and chart the post-lockdown landscape must include: how can schools adopt systems that aid remote learning generally, and how can we tackle the demands of meeting pastoral needs specifically?

Perhaps a more pressing concern is how schools will plan for re-opening. Such a seemingly simple idea raises significant questions in terms of the logistics of maintaining social distancing and keeping students, teachers and other staff members safe. The matter is complicated further by the ongoing uncertainty about which year groups will return and when. Meanwhile, what might be the pastoral needs of a school community trying to operate whilst fragmented and still living under the shadow of fear that an ongoing global pandemic inevitably casts? Questions about how the transition from Year 6 to Year 7 will operate have become of immediate concern in my role, along with finding ways to support Year 9 students as they face an anxious wait to begin Year 10. It seems unlikely that we will be back to business as usual by the start of the new academic year. Meanwhile, the Year 10s are preparing to embark on their final year of GCSEs without any certainty about how their examinations might be affected, and Year 12 students face similar uncertainties about how Year 13 will play out. For Year 13 students who may be hoping to start university in the autumn, the lack of clarity may well be daunting.

Whatever else this crisis may have shown us, it has become clear that 'education' is not the only - or even the primary - purpose of schooling. Rather, it is the four Cs of the pastoral that form the core purpose of school: care, curriculum, cultivation and congregation.

Some possible suggestions might include:

- Ensure that you have up-to-date contact details for every child.
- Consider communication methods that enable students to keep in touch as well as parents.
- Use closed social networks to foster an ongoing sense of community. Provide technological support where needed, if possible, or adopt alternative strategies for families without access.
- Continue to deliver assemblies and other pastoral content as well as academic content.
- Encourage students to engage with outdoor learning where possible, but be mindful that not all students have access to outside space.

- Develop communication protocols that ensure all students can be contacted on a weekly basis during extended school closures.
- Find mechanisms for sharing examples of work and activities amongst the school community.
- Look after each other.

Conclusion

In Chapter 1 I set out to consider some questions around how to develop an informed approach to enacting the role of pastoral leader in a school, whether this be as form tutor, head of year or other middle leadership role, or senior leader. I did not intend, necessarily, to answer those questions, but to present my own reflections on the journey of becoming more informed, of moving away from mere practice towards deliberate, thoughtful praxis.

Pastoral roles are difficult to properly define, despite having a sense of 'everyone knows' about them. Job descriptions do not really help; attempts to codify the nebulous nature of the pastoral seem to end up resting upon administrative functions and struggle to encapsulate the more ethereal, conceptual and theoretical aspects.

There is a lack of specific discussion of the pastoral in the increasingly popular research-informed 'what works' discourse, despite increasing focus from government and the inspectorate on personal development, mental health and wellbeing. Indeed, the 'what works' discourse often seems to eschew any theory which isn't CLT!

There are still important debates to be had about the purposes of schooling, and I don't think 'to make kids cleverer' is necessarily enough, unless 'making kids clever' can include all of the dimensions considered in Chapter 3 - making kids cleverer about themselves, about the world and about each other. There is much more philosophical thinking to be done here. Seeing school as an act of *Bildung* could shift the focus away from the exam-results-oriented, target-driven, deliverology model of teaching and learning towards a more human, more humane, socially aware quest for wisdom - Robinson's (2019) Athena. If we could envisage schools as operating in pursuit of wisdom, I think we could conceive of a radically different experience for our students.

Such a view might help us to reconceptualise our ideas about curriculum, especially the pastoral curriculum. Schools need to do much more work on developing a cohesive pastoral curriculum that takes students on a learning journey, just as they might do for subject disciplines or domains. Such a pastoral curriculum should be built around the core elements of knowledge that we would want children to learn, developing a spiral approach which regularly revisits and builds upon prior learning. But it would also require teachers and leaders to be much more deliberate in their planning and delivery of assemblies, and of the messages that are communicated in all our encounters – in the corridors, in disciplining students, at the doors of our classrooms and so on. These messages should form golden threads which all staff in the school can articulate, repeat and incorporate into their daily discourses with each other and with students.

There is general discontent with the CPD that is provided for teachers. Essentially, it is woeful; school INSET is generally administrative, dealing mostly with top-down messages and worrying about what inspectors might be looking for. School leaders should take a good hard look at their CPD. It is not enough to simply remind staff about the core expectations every half-term. A genuine knowledge-rich school should take the curriculum for its staff seriously. And teachers must be encouraged to engage in the theoretical and philosophical debates around teaching in order to continually test their practice, and so move it towards daily praxis. Why are we doing what we are doing? How do we know it works? What does 'works' look like for us?

These kinds of questions should lead to a review of policy and practice in schools. It could well be recommended that leaders reconsider their school policy documents with regard to the pastoral. What evidence or theoretical positions are you calling upon in your behaviour policy and your anti-bullying policy? Perhaps the most important place to start is with your pastoral curriculum – do you have a cohesive pastoral curriculum that unifies the obviously taught aspects of PSHE education and citizenship with the key messages that you wish to communicate? Does your curriculum unhide and make explicit the usually more tacit knowledge that your students are expected to possess? If it does, congratulations. If it does not, I hope these chapters have given you food for thought.

References and Further Reading

Ainsworth, M. D. S., Blehar, M. C., Waters, E. and Wall, S. (1978) *Patterns of Attachment: A Psychological Study of the Strange Situation*. Hillsdale, NJ: Lawrence Erlbaum Associates.

Almond, N. (2019) Ramble #6 Achieving coherence in primary science (Why primary Science needs to be less like the Simpsons and more like Game of Thrones). *Nuts About Teaching* [blog] (4 January). Available at: https://nutsaboutteaching.wordpress.com/2019/01/04/ramble-6-achieving-coherence-in-primary-science-why-primary-science-needs-to-be-less-like-the-simpsons-and-more-like-game-of-thrones.

Ansell, C. and Geyer, R. (2017) 'Pragmatic complexity' a new foundation for moving beyond 'evidence-based policy making'? *Policy Studies*, 38(2): 149-167. DOI: 10.1080/01442872.2016.1219033

Arnold, M. (1869) *Culture and Anarchy: An Essay in Political and Social Criticism*. Project Gutenberg edn. Available at: http://www.gutenberg.org/ebooks/4212.

Arthur, J. and O'Shaugnessy, J. (2012) Character and Attainment: Does Character Make the Grade? Available at: https://www.jubileecentre.ac.uk/userfiles/jubileecentre/pdf/other-centre-papers/Arthur_2012_Character and Attainment.pdf.

Augustine, C., Engberg, J., Grimm, G., Lee, E., Lin Wang, E., Christianson, K. and Joseph, A. A. (2018) Can Restorative Practices Improve School Climate and Curb Suspensions? An Evaluation of the Impact of Restorative Practices in a Mid-Sized Urban School District. Available at: https://www.rand.org/pubs/research_reports/RR2840.html.

Babad, E. Y., Inbar, J. and Rosenthal, R. (1982) Pygmalion, Galatea, and the Golem: investigations of biased and unbiased teachers. *Journal of Educational Psychology*, 74(4): 459-474. DOI: 10.1037/0022-0663.74.4.459

BACP (2015) *School Counselling for All*. British Association for Counselling and Psychotherapy: Lutterworth. Available at: https://www.bacp.co.uk/media/2127/bacp-school-based-counselling-for-all-briefing-dec15.pdf.

Baehr, J. (2017) The varieties of character and some implications for character education. *Journal of Youth and Adolescence*, 46(6): 1153-1161. DOI: 10.1007/s10964-017-0654-z

Ball, S. J. (2012) *Global Education Inc: New Policy Networks and the Neoliberal Imaginary*, 1st edn. Abingdon and New York: Routledge.

Ball, S. J. (2012) The reluctant state and the beginning of the end of state education. *Journal of Educational Administration and History*, 44(2): 89-103.

Ball, S. J. (2015) Living the neo-liberal university. *European Journal of Education*, 50(3): 258-261. DOI: 10.1111/ejed.12132

Ball, S. J. and Junemann, C. (2012) *Networks, New Governance and Education*. Bristol: The Policy Press.

Barrow, G. (2019) Being well in the world: an alternative discourse to mental health and well-being. *Pastoral Care in Education*, 37(1): 26-32. DOI: 10.1080/02643944.2019.1569845

BBC News (2018) Ninestiles school to enforce 'silent corridor' rule (28 October). Available at: https://www.bbc.co.uk/news/uk-england-birmingham-45931847.

BBC News (2020) Caroline Flack: 'Be kind,' social-media users urge (17 February). Available at: https://www.bbc.co.uk/news/blogs-trending-51532841.

BCU (2019) Zero tolerance policies cause anger not reflection. *Birmingham City University* (12 April). Available at: https://www.bcu.ac.uk/education-and-social-work/about-us/news-and-events/zero-tolerance-policies-cause-anger-not-reflection.

Bennett, T. (2017) *Creating a Culture: How School Leaders Can Optimise Behaviour* [Bennett Report]. Ref: DFE-00059-2017. London: Department for Education. Available at: https://www.gov.uk/government/uploads/system/uploads/attachment_data/file/602487/Tom_Bennett_Independent_Review_of_Behaviour_in_Schools.pdf.

Bennett, T. (2019) The Beginning Teacher's Behaviour Toolkit: A Summary. London: Department for Education. Available at: https://assets.publishing.service.gov.uk/government/uploads/system/uploads/attachment_data/file/844181/_Tom_Bennett_summary.pdf.

Bergeron, P-J. (2017) How to engage in pseudoscience with real data: a criticism of John Hattie's arguments in *Visible Learning* from the perspective of a statistician, tr. L. Rivard. *McGill Journal of Education*, 52(1): 237-246. Available at: https://mje.mcgill.ca/article/view/9475/7229.

Bergin, C. and Bergin, D. (2009) Attachment in the Classroom. *Educational Psychology Review*, 21(2): 141-170. DOI: 10.1007/s10648-009-9104-0

Berry, K., Bucci, S. and Danquah, A. N. (2020) *Attachment Theory and Psychosis: Current Perspectives and Future Directions*. Abingdon and New York: Routledge.

Best, R. (2014) Forty years of *Pastoral Care*: an appraisal of Michael Marland's seminal book and its significance for pastoral care in schools. *Pastoral Care in Education*, 32(3): 173-185. DOI: 10.1080/02643944.2014.951385

Best, R. (2019) Can I tell you about self-harm? A guide for friends, family and professionals. *Pastoral Care in Education*, 37(1): 81-82, DOI: 10.1080/02643944.2019.1582841

Betts, L. R., Gkimitzoudis, A., Spenser, K. A. and Baguley, T. (2016) Examining the roles young people fulfill in five types of cyber bullying. *Journal of Social and Personal Relationships*, 34(7): 1080-1098. DOI: 10.1177/0265407516668585

Biesta, G. (2015) What is education for? On good education, teacher judgement, and educational professionalism. *European Journal of Education*, 50(1): 75-87. DOI: 10.1111/ejed.12109

Biesta, G. (2016) *The Beautiful Risk of Education. Interventions: Education, Philosophy, and Culture*. Abingdon and New York: Routledge.

Bowlby, J. (2005 [1979]) *The Making and Breaking of Affectional Bonds*. Abingdon and New York: Routledge.

Bowlby, J. (2008 [1988]) *A Secure Base: Clinical Applications of Attachment Theory*. Abingdon and New York: Routledge.

Brunon-Ernst, A. (ed.) (2016) *Beyond Foucault: New Perspectives on Bentham's Panopticon*. Abingdon and New York: Routledge.

Burke, M. and Lehain, M. (2018) Clogging up the Classroom – the Jostle for Curriculum Content. Available at: https://parentsandteachers.org.uk/wp-content/uploads/2019/03/20181221_-_WSST_-_Clogging_up_the_classroom.pdf.

Busby, E. (2019) Protests against LGBT+ lessons permanently banned from outside Birmingham primary school, *The Independent* (26 November). Available at: https://www.independent.co.uk/news/education/education-news/birmingham-lgbt-protest-ban-school-same-sex-education-court-ruling-a9218101.html.

Calvert, M. (2009) From 'pastoral care' to 'care': meanings and practices. *Pastoral Care in Education*, 27(4): 267–277. DOI: 10.1080/02643940903349302

Carnell, E. and Lodge, C. (2002) Support for students' learning: what the form tutor can do. *Pastoral Care in Education*, 20(4): 12–20. DOI: 10.1111/1468-0122.00239

Casey, B. J. and Caudle, K. (2013) The teenage brain: self control. *Current Directions in Psychological Science*, 22(2): 82–87. DOI: 10.1177/0963721413480170

Chamberlain, Z. (2019) Teachers to strike at 'outstanding' school where 'violent pupils carry knives', *Birmingham Live* (26 June). Available at: https://www.birminghammail.co.uk/news/midlands-news/teachers-strike-outside-outstanding-school-16492073.

Clark, B. R. E., Kirschner, P. A. and Sweller, J. (2012) Putting students on the path to learning: the case for fully guided instruction. *American Educator*, Spring: 6–11. Available at: http://www.aft.org/sites/default/files/periodicals/Clark.pdf.

Clarke, E. and Visser, J. (2019) Pragmatic research methodology in education: possibilities and pitfalls. *International Journal of Research & Method in Education*, 42(5): 455–469. DOI: 10.1080/1743727X.2018.1524866

Claxton, G. and Lucas, B. (2015) *Educating Ruby: What Our Children Really Need to Learn*. Carmarthen: Crown House Publishing.

Claxton, G. and Lucas, B. (2016) The hole in the heart of education pedagogy (and the role of psychology in addressing it). *Psychology of Education Review*, 40(1): 4–12. Available at: https://www.researchgate.net/publication/301635707.

Connolly, P., Keenan, C. and Urbanska, K. (2018) The trials of evidence-based practice in education: a systematic review of randomised controlled trials in education research 1980–2016, *Educational Research*, 60(3): 276–291. DOI: 10.1080/00131881.2018.1493353

Corngold, J. (2013) Introduction: the ethics of sex education. *Educational Theory*, 63(5): 439–442. DOI: 10.1111/edth.12033

Cotton, D., Winter, J. and Bailey, I. (2013) Researching the hidden curriculum: intentional and unintended messages. *Journal of Geography in Higher Education*, 37(2): 192–203. DOI: 10.1080/03098265.2012.733684

Coughlan, S. (2019a) Child, four, among pupils taking weapons to school. *BBC News* (16 October). Available at: https://www.bbc.co.uk/news/education-50056275.

Coughlan, S. (2019b) 'Sadfishing' social media warning from school heads, *BBC News* (1 October). Available at: https://www.bbc.co.uk/news/education-49883030.

Counsell, C. (2018) Senior curriculum leadership 1: the indirect manifestation of knowledge: (a) curriculum as narrative. *The Dignity of the Thing* [blog] (7 April). Available at: https://thedignityofthethingblog.wordpress.com/2018/04/07/senior-curriculum-leadership-1-the-indirect-manifestation-of-knowledge-a-curriculum-as-narrative.

Cowley, S. (2010) *Getting the Buggers to Behave*, 4th edn. London and New York: Continuum.

Curtis, A. J. (2014) Tracing the school-to-prison pipeline from zero-tolerance policies to juvenile justice dispositions. *Georgetown Law Journal*, 102(4): 1251-1277.

Daniels, P. (ed.) (2009) *Zero Tolerance Policies in Schools*. Detroit, MI: Greenhaven Press.

Davies, E. L. (2016) 'The monster of the month': teachers' views about alcohol within personal, social, health, and economic education (PSHE) in schools. *Drugs and Alcohol Today*, 16(4): 279-288. DOI: 10.1108/DAT-02-2016-0005

Department for Education (2016) *Counselling in Schools: A Blueprint for the Future: Departmental Advice for School Leaders and Counsellors*. Ref: DFE-00117-2015. Available at: https://assets.publishing.service.gov.uk/government/uploads/system/uploads/attachment_data/file/497825/Counselling_in_schools.pdf.

Department for Education (2017) *Preventing and Tackling Bullying: Advice for Head Teachers, Staff and Governing Bodies*. Ref: DFE-00160-2017. Available at: https://assets.publishing.service.gov.uk/government/uploads/system/uploads/attachment_data/file/623895/Preventing_and_tackling_bullying_advice.pdf.

Department for Education (2019a) Character and Resilience: A Call for Evidence (launched 27 May). Available at: https://consult.education.gov.uk/character-citizenship-cadets-team/character-and-resilience-a-call-for-evidence/supporting_documents/Character%20and%20Resilience%20Call%20for%20Evidence.pdf.

Department for Education (2019b) *Character Education Framework Guidance*. Ref: DfE-00235-2019. Available at: https://assets.publishing.service.gov.uk/government/uploads/system/uploads/attachment_data/file/849654/Character_Education_Framework_Guidance.pdf.

Department for Education (2019c) *Keeping Children Safe in Education: Statutory Guidance for Schools and Colleges*. Ref: DFE-00129-2019. Available at: https://assets.publishing.service.gov.uk/government/uploads/system/uploads/attachment_data/file/835733/Keeping_children_safe_in_education_2019.pdf.

Department for Education (2019d) Permanent and Fixed-Period Exclusions in England: 2017 to 2018 [statistical release]. Available at: https://assets.publishing.service.gov.uk/government/uploads/system/uploads/attachment_data/file/820773/Permanent_and_fixed_period_exclusions_2017_to_2018_-_main_text.pdf.

Department for Education (2019e) *Relationships Education, Relationships and Sex Education (RSE) and Health Education: Statutory Guidance for Governing Bodies, Proprietors, Head Teachers, Principals, Senior Leadership Teams, Teachers*. Available at: https://assets.publishing.service.gov.uk/government/uploads/system/uploads/attachment_data/file/805781/Relationships_

Education__Relationships_and_Sex_Education__RSE__and_Health_
Education.pdf.

Department for Education and Gibb, N. (2015) Nick Gibb: the importance of the teaching profession [transcript] (5 September). Available at: https://www.gov.uk/government/speeches/nick-gibb-the-importance-of-the-teaching-profession.

Department for Education and Gibb, N. (2018) School standards minister at researchED [transcript] (8 September). Available at: https://www.gov.uk/government/speeches/school-standards-minister-at-researched.

Department for Education and Hinds, D. (2019a) All pupils will be taught about mental and physical wellbeing [press release] (25 February). Available at: https://www.gov.uk/government/news/all-pupils-will-be-taught-about-mental-and-physical-wellbeing.

Department for Education and Hinds, D. (2019b) Education secretary sets out five foundations to build character [transcript] (7 January). Available at: https://www.gov.uk/government/speeches/education-secretary-sets-out-five-foundations-to-build-character.

Department of Education and Science (1989) *The Elton Report: Discipline in Schools*. London: Her Majesty's Stationery Office. Available at: http://www.educationengland.org.uk/documents/elton/elton1989.html.

Department of Health (2015) *Future in Mind: Promoting, Protecting and Improving Our Children and Young People's Mental Health and Wellbeing*. NHS England Publication Gateway Ref. No 02939. Available at: https://assets.publishing.service.gov.uk/government/uploads/system/uploads/attachment_data/file/414024/Childrens_Mental_Health.pdf.

Department of Health and Department for Education (2017) *Transforming Children and Young People's Mental Health Provision: A Green Paper*. Available at: https://assets.publishing.service.gov.uk/government/uploads/system/uploads/attachment_data/file/664855/Transforming_children_and_young_people_s_mental_health_provision.pdf.

Dewar, G. (2019) The effects of praise: 7 evidence-based tips for using praise wisely. *Parenting Science*. Available at: https://www.parentingscience.com/effects-of-praise.html.

Didau, D. (2015) *What If Everything You Knew About Education Was Wrong?* Carmarthen: Crown House Publishing.

Dix, P. (2017) *When the Adults Change, Everything Changes: Seismic Shifts in School Behaviour*. Carmarthen: Independent Thinking Press.

Dupper, D. R. (2013) *School Bullying: New Perspectives on a Growing Problem*. New York: Oxford University Press.

Espelage, D. L., Rao, M. A. and De La Rue, L. (2013) Current research on school-based bullying: a social-ecological perspective. *Journal of Social Distress and the Homeless*, 22(1): 21–27. DOI: 10.1179/1053078913Z.0000000002

Fan, W. and Wolters, C. A. (2014) School motivation and high school dropout: the mediating role of educational expectation. *British Journal of Educational Psychology*, 84(1): 22–39. DOI: 10.1111/bjep.12002

Ferguson, D. (2019) 'We can't give in': the Birmingham school on the frontline of anti-LGBT protests. *The Guardian* (26 May). Available at: https://www.

theguardian.com/uk-news/2019/may/26/birmingham-anderton-park-primary-muslim-protests-lgbt-teaching-rights.

Foucault, M. (1980) *Power/Knowledge: Selected Interviews and Other Writings, 1972-1977*, ed. C. Gordon. London: Pantheon.

Foucault, M. (1991) *Discipline and Punish: The Birth of the Prison*, tr. A. Sheridan. New York: Vintage.

Foucault, M. (1997) Self writing. In *Ethics, Subjectivity and Truth: The Essential Works of Foucault, 1954-1984*, vol. 1, ed. P. Rabinow. New York: The New Press, pp. 207-222.

George, M. (2018) Exclusive: no excuses schools are 'like workhouses'. *TES* (29 June). Available at: https://www.tes.com/news/exclusive-no-excuses-schools-workhouses.

Gillen-O'Neel, C. and Fuligni, A. (2012) A longitudinal study of school belonging and academic motivation across high school. *Child Development*, 84(2): 678-692. DOI: 10.1111/j.1467-8624.2012.01862.x

Glazzard, J. and Bancroft, K. (2018) *Meeting the Mental Health Needs of Learners 11-18 Years*. St Albans: Critical Publishing.

Golann, J. W. (2015) The paradox of success at a no-excuses school. *American Sociological Association*, 88(2): 103-119. DOI: 10.1177/0038040714567866

Goldacre, B. (2013) Building Evidence into Education (March). Available at: http://media.education.gov.uk/assets/files/pdf/b/ben%20goldacre%20paper.pdf.

Gove, M. (2012) How are the children? Achievement for all in the 21st century [transcript] (27 June). Available at: http://www.education.gov.uk/inthenews/speeches/a00210738/govespect.

Gregory, A. and Cornell, D. (2009) 'Tolerating' adolescent needs: moving beyond zero tolerance policies in high school. *Theory into Practice*, 48(2): 106-113. DOI: 10.1080/00405840902776327

Hallgarten, L. (2020) Forging a new generation of sexually healthy young people. *Terrence Higgins Trust* [blog] (14 February). Available at: https://www.tht.org.uk/news/forging-new-generation-sexually-healthy-young-people.

Hand, M. (2013) Framing classroom discussion of same-sex marriage. *Educational Theory*, 63(5): 497-510. DOI: 10.1111/edth.12037

Hart, R. (2010) Classroom behaviour management: educational psychologists' views on effective practice. *Emotional and Behavioural Difficulties*, 15(4): 353-371. DOI: 10.1080/13632752.2010.523257

Hattie, J. (2008) *Visible Learning: A Synthesis of Over 800 Meta-Analyses Relating to Achievement*. Abingdon and New York: Routledge.

Hill, M. S. (2017) Impact of perfectionism on students: the good, the bad, and the indifferent. *NACADA* (25 May). Available at: https://nacada.ksu.edu/Resources/Academic-Advising-Today/View-Articles/Impact-of-Perfectionism-on-Students-The-Good-the-Bad-and-the-Indifferent.aspx.

Hirsch, E. D. (2013) Primer on success: character and knowledge make the difference. *Education Next*, 13(1). Available at: https://www.educationnext.org/primer-on-success/#.

Hodgson, N., Vlieghe, J. and Zamojski, P. (2017) *Manifesto for a Post-Critical Pedagogy*. Santa Barbara, CA: Punctum.

Hodgson, N., Vlieghe, J. and Zamojski, P. (2018) Education and the love for the world: articulating a post-critical educational philosophy. *Foro de Educación*,

16(24): 7–20. Available at: http://www.forodeeducacion.com/ojs/index.php/fde/article/view/576/396Hod.

Hodis, F. A., Meyer, L. H., McClure, J., Weir, K. F. and Walkey, F. H. (2011) A longitudinal investigation of motivation and secondary school achievement using growth mixture modeling. *Journal of Educational Psychology*, 103(2): 312–323. DOI: 10.1037/a0022547

Holmes, J. (2014) *John Bowlby and Attachment Theory: Makers of Modern Psychotherapy*, 2nd edn. Abingdon and New York: Routledge.

Humanists UK (2019) Humanists UK welcomes compulsory home-school register as move to shut down illegal schools (2 April). Available at: https://humanism.org.uk/2019/04/02/humanists-uk-welcomes-compulsory-home-school-register-as-move-to-shut-down-illegal-schools/.

Illich, I. (1971) *Deschooling Society*. New York: Harper & Row.

Ing, E. (2018) Vocational qualifications, Progress 8 and 'gaming'. *Ofsted Blog: Schools, Early Years, Further Education and Skills* [blog] (4 September). Available at: https://educationinspection.blog.gov.uk/2018/09/04/vocational-qualifications-progress-8-and-gaming/.

Issimdar, M. (2018) Homeschooling in the UK increases 40% over three years, *BBC News* (26 April). Available at: https://www.bbc.co.uk/news/uk-england-42624220.

Jackson, P. (1968) *Life in Classrooms*. New York: Holt, Rinehart and Winston.

James, D., Flynn, A., Lawlor, M., Murphy, N. and Henry, B. (2011) A friend in deed? Can adolescent girls be taught to understand relational bullying? *Child Abuse Review*, 20(6): 439–454. DOI: 10.1002/car.1120

Jargon, J. (2019) Sadfishing, predators and bullies: the hazards of being 'real' on social media. *Wall Street Journal* (12 November). Available at: https://www.wsj.com/articles/sadfishing-predators-and-bullies-the-hazards-of-being-real-on-social-media-11573554603.

Jones, P. (2019) National guidance for pastoral support in schools. *NAPCE* (3 April). Available at: https://www.napce.org.uk/national-guidance-for-pastoral-support-in-schools/.

Jubilee Centre for Character and Virtues (2017) *A Framework for Character Education in Schools*. Birmingham: University of Birmingham. Available at: https://uobschool.org.uk/wp-content/uploads/2017/08/Framework-for-Character-Education-2017-Jubilee-Centre.pdf.

Jubilee Centre for Character and Virtues (2019) Department for Education Re-launches National Character Awards (19 July). Available at: https://www.jubileecentre.ac.uk/media/news/article/5626/Department-for-Education-Re-launches-National-Character-Awards.

Kershen, J. L., Weiner, J. M. and Torres, C. (2019) Control as care: how teachers in 'no excuses' charter schools position their students and themselves. *Equity and Excellence in Education*, 51(3–4): 265–283. DOI: 10.1080/10665684.2018.1539359

Kirby, J. (2016) No excuses: high standards, high support. *Pragmatic Reform* [blog] (10 December). Available at: https://pragmaticreform.wordpress.com/2016/12/10/no-excuses-high-standards-high-support/.

Knight, K., Gibson, K. L. and Cartwright, C. (2018) 'It's like a refuge': young people's relationships with school counsellors. *Counselling and Psychotherapy Research*, 18(4): 377–386. DOI: 10.1002/capr.12186

Kohn, A. (2005) *Unconditional Parenting: Moving from Rewards and Punishments to Love and Reason*. New York: Simon & Schuster.

Kohn, A. (2012) Criticizing (common criticisms of) praise. *Alfie Kohn* [blog] (3 February). Available at: https://www.alfiekohn.org/blogs/criticizing-common-criticisms-praise.

Kohn, A. (2018) *Punished by Rewards: The Trouble with Gold Stars, Incentive Plans, A's, Praise, and Other Bribes*, 25th anniversary edn. Boston, MA: Houghton Mifflin Harcourt.

Kristjánsson, K. (2013) Ten myths about character, virtue and virtue education – plus three well-founded misgivings. *British Journal of Educational Studies*, 61(3): 269–287. DOI: 10.1080/00071005.2013.778386

Kyriacou, C. and Zuin, A. (2018) Cyberbullying bystanders and moral engagement: a psychosocial analysis for pastoral care. *Pastoral Care in Education*, 36(2): 99–111. DOI: 10.1080/02643944.2018.1453857

Lamb, S. (2013) Just the facts? The separation of sex education from moral education. *Educational Theory*, 63(5): 443–460. DOI: 10.1111/edth.12034

Lamblin, M., Murawski, C., Whittle, S. and Fornito, A. (2017) Social connectedness, mental health and the adolescent brain. *Neuroscience and Biobehavioral Reviews*, 80: 57–68. DOI: 10.1016/j.neubiorev.2017.05.010

Lane, S. (2016) Need vs entitlement. *Sputniksteve* [blog] (10 August). Available at: https://sputniksteve.wordpress.com/2016/08/10/need-vs-entitlement/.

Lehain, M. (2019) Why all schools should be 'warm-strict' on behaviour. *TES* (6 September). Available at: https://www.tes.com/news/why-all-schools-should-be-warm-strict-behaviour.

Lemov, D. (2010) *Teach Like a Champion: 49 Techniques That Put Students on the Path to College*. San Francisco, CA: Jossey-Bass.

Lemov, D. (2015) *Teach Like a Champion 2.0: 62 Techniques That Put Students on the Path to College*. San Francisco, CA: Jossey-Bass.

Leroy, M-L. (2016) Transparency and politics: the reversed Panopticon as a response to abuse of power. In A. Brunon-Ernst (ed.), *Beyond Foucault: New Perspectives on Bentham's Panopticon*. Abingdon and New York: Routledge, pp. 143–160.

Levine, E. and Tamburrino, M. (2014) Bullying among young children: strategies for prevention. *Early Childhood Education*, 42(4): 271–278. DOI: 10.1007/s10643-013-0600-y

Lodge, C. (2008) Beyond the head of year. *Pastoral Care in Education*, 24(1): 4–9. DOI: 10.1111/j.1468-0122.2005.00355.x

Lord, A. (2019) School isolation is hurting a generation of young people. *Vice*. (21 May). Available at: https://www.vice.com/en_uk/article/7xg4v9/school-isolation-is-hurting-a-generation-of-young-people.

Lord, E. (1983) Pastoral care in education: principles and practice. *Pastoral Care in Education*, 1(1): 6–11. DOI: 10.1080/02643948309470414

Lubienski, C., Puckett, T. and Brewer, T. J. (2013) Does homeschooling 'work'? A critique of the empirical claims and agenda of advocacy organizations. *Peabody Journal of Education*, 88(3): 378–392. DOI: 10.1080/0161956X.2013.798516

Lucas, B. and Spencer, E. (2017) *Teaching Creative Thinking: Developing Learners Who Generate Ideas and Can Think Critically*. Carmarthen: Crown House Publishing.

Lucas, B. and Spencer, E. (2018) *Developing Tenacity: Teaching Learners How to Persevere in the Face of Difficulty*. Carmarthen: Crown House Publishing.

McCarthy, R. (2019) As a teenager, I believe our mental health is harmed by this dehumanising education system. *The Independent* (24 August). Available at: https://www.independent.co.uk/voices/young-people-teenagers-mental-health-university-gcse-grades-depression-a9077556.html.

McCluskey, G., Lloyd, G., Kane, J., Riddell, S. and Stead, J. (2008) Can restorative practices in schools make a difference? *Educational Review*, 60(4): 405–417. DOI: 10.1080/00131910802393456

McInerney, L. (2018) What if it's behaviour, not workload, that makes teachers leave? *Schools Week* (24 September). Available at: https://schoolsweek.co.uk/what-if-its-behaviour-not-workload-that-makes-teachers-leave.

McKnight, L. and Whitburn, B. (2020) Seven reasons to question the hegemony of *Visible Learning*. *Discourse: Studies in the Cultural Politics of Education*, 41(1): 32–44. DOI: 10.1080/01596306.2018.1480474

McMullan, T. (2015) What does the panopticon mean in the age of digital surveillance? *The Guardian* (23 July). Available at: https://www.theguardian.com/technology/2015/jul/23/panopticon-digital-surveillance-jeremy-bentham.

Mahon, K., Heikkinen, H. L. T. and Huttunen, R. (2018) Critical educational praxis in university ecosystems: enablers and constraints. *Pedagogy, Culture and Society*, 27(3): 463–480. DOI: 10.1080/14681366.2018.1522663

Marland, M. (1974) *Pastoral Care*. London: Heinemann.

Mishna, F. (2012) *Bullying: A Guide to Research, Intervention, and Prevention*. New York: Oxford University Press.

Moore, T. C., Maggin, D. M., Thompson, K. M., Gordon, J., Daniels, S. and Lang, L. (2019) Evidence review for teacher praise to improve students' classroom behavior. *Journal of Positive Behavior Interventions*, 21(1): 3–18. DOI: 10.1177/1098300718766657

Murray, C. (2019) No evidence for 'no excuses' behaviour policies. *Schools Week* (16 February). Available at: https://schoolsweek.co.uk/no-evidence-for-no-excuses-behaviour-policies.

Nassem, E. (2019) *The Teacher's Guide to Resolving School Bullying: Evidence-Based Strategies and Pupil-Led Interventions*. London: Jessica Kingsley Publishers.

Neville, B. (2013) The enchanted loom. In M. Newberry, A. Gallant and P. Riley (eds), *Emotion and School: Understanding How the Hidden Curriculum Influences Relationships, Leadership, Teaching, and Learning*, Advances in Research on Teaching, vol. 18. Bingley: Emerald Group Publishing Limited, pp. 3–23.

Newmark, B. (2019) Why teach? *BENNEWMARK* [blog] (10 February). Available at: https://bennewmark.wordpress.com/2019/02/10/why-teach/.

NHS Digital (2018) Mental Health of Children and Young People in England, 2017: Summary of Key Findings [official statistics], p. 8. Available at: https://files.digital.nhs.uk/A6/EA7D58/MHCYP%202017%20Summary.pdf.

Norris, H. (2019) The impact of restorative approaches on well-being: an evaluation of happiness and engagement in schools. *Conflict Resolution Quarterly*, 36(3): 221–234. DOI: 10.1002/crq.21242

Nuffield Health (2018a) *Improving Wellbeing in Schools: Evidence and Recommendations from a 'Head of Wellbeing' Pilot*. Available at: https://www.nuffieldhealth.com/about-us/our-impact/our-projects/schools-wellbeing.

Nuffield Health (2018b) Wellbeing in schools pilot [video] (10 October). Available at: https://www.youtube.com/watch?v=dFECc-fVbeM.

O'Shaughnessy, J. (2015) Knowledge and character. In J. Simons and N. Porter (eds), *Knowledge and the Curriculum: A Collection of Essays to Accompany E. D. Hirsch's Lecture at Policy Exchange*. London: Policy Exchange, pp. 29–35.

Ofqual (2019) Entries for GCSE, AS and A Level Summer 2019 Exam Series [official statistics]. Available at: https://assets.publishing.service.gov.uk/government/uploads/system/uploads/attachment_data/file/803906/Provisional_entries_for_GCSE__AS_and_A_level_summer_2019_exam_series.pdf.

Ofsted (2013) *Not Yet Good Enough: Personal, Social, Health and Economic Education in Schools*. Ref: 130065. Available at: https://assets.publishing.service.gov.uk/government/uploads/system/uploads/attachment_data/file/413178/Not_yet_good_enough_personal__social__health_and_economic_education_in_schools.pdf.

Ofsted (2014) *Below the Radar: Low-Level Disruption in the Country's Classrooms*. Ref: 140157. Available at: https://www.gov.uk/government/publications/below-the-radar-low-level-disruption-in-the-countrys-classrooms.

Ofsted (2019a) *School Inspection Handbook*. Ref: 190017. Available at: https://assets.publishing.service.gov.uk/government/uploads/system/uploads/attachment_data/file/843108/School_inspection_handbook_-_section_5.pdf.

Ofsted (2019b) *The Education Inspection Framework*. Ref: 190015. Available at: https://assets.publishing.service.gov.uk/government/uploads/system/uploads/attachment_data/file/801429/Education_inspection_framework.pdf.

Ofsted and Schooling, E. (2017) Social care commentary: hidden children – the challenges of safeguarding children who are not attending school. *Gov.uk* (21 December). Available at: https://www.gov.uk/government/speeches/social-care-commentary-hidden-children-the-challenges-of-safeguarding-children-who-are-not-attending-school.

Ofsted and Spielman, A. (2019) HMCI commentary: managing behaviour research. *Gov.uk* (12 September). Available at: https://www.gov.uk/government/speeches/research-commentary-managing-behaviour.

Oliver, A. and Farmer, L. (2019) Case study: reflective conversations, peer mediation and a restorative ethos. *SecEd* (13 March). Available at: http://www.sec-ed.co.uk/best-practice/case-study-reflective-conversations-peer-mediation-and-a-restorative-ethos/.

Pattison, S. (2008) Is pastoral care dead in a mission-led church? *Practical Theology*, 1(1): 7–10. DOI: 10.1558/prth.v1i1.7

Pavey, H. (2017) Kinder eggs go back on sale in the US – almost 50 years after they were banned. *Evening Standard* (15 November). Available at: https://www.standard.co.uk/news/world/the-us-is-finally-lifting-its-ban-on-kinder-eggs-a3691696.html.

Payne, R. (2015) Using rewards and sanctions in the classroom: pupils' perceptions of their own responses to current behaviour management strategies. *Educational Review*, 67(4): 483–504. DOI: 10.1080/00131911.2015.1008407

Perraudin, F. (2018) Use of isolation booths in schools criticised as 'barbaric' punishment. *The Guardian* (2 September). Available at: https://www. theguardian.com/education/2018/sep/02/barbaric-school-punishment-of-consequence-rooms-criticised-by-parents.

Perraudin, F. (2019) Mother sues over daughter's suicide attempt in school isolation booth. *The Guardian* (2 April). Available at: https://www.theguardian. com/education/2019/apr/03/isolation-of-children-at-academies-prompts-legal-action.

Perryman, J. and Calvert, G. (2020) What motivates people to teach, and why do they leave? Accountability, performativity and teacher retention. *British Journal of Educational Studies*, 68(1): 3–23. DOI: 10.1080/00071005.2019.1589417

Peterson, A., Lexmond, J., Hallgarten, J. and Kerr, D. (2014) *Schools with Soul: A New Approach to Spiritual, Moral, Social and Cultural Education Contents.* London: RSA. Available at: https://www.thersa.org/globalassets/pdfs/reports/ schools-with-soul-report.pdf.

Petty, G. (2009) *Evidence-Based Teaching*, 2nd edn. Cheltenham: Nelson Thornes.

Pivotal Education (2016) The Pivotal approach to behaviour management [video] (19 February). Available at: https://www.youtube.com/watch?v=ZTx02PdLSDs.

Policy Exchange (2014) Teaching character education in schools is a waste of time [video] (4 November). Available at: https://www.youtube.com/ watch?v=DFQX5pr_7jQ.

Porter, J. (2016) No excuses discipline works. *Michaela Community School* [blog] (24 April). Available at: https://mcsbrent.co.uk/humanities-24-04-2016-no-excuses-discipline-works.

Porter, L. (2014) *Behaviour in Schools: Theory and Practice for Teachers*, 3rd edn. Maidenhead: Open University Press.

Public Health England (2019) People urged to practise safer sex after rise in STIs in England [press release] (4 June). Available at: https://www.gov.uk/ government/news/people-urged-to-practise-safer-sex-after-rise-in-stis-in-england.

Qualifications and Curriculum Authority (1998) *Education for Citizenship and the Teaching of Democracy in Schools: Final Report of the Advisory Group on Citizenship* [The Crick Report]. London: Qualifications and Curriculum Authority. Available at: https://dera.ioe.ac.uk/4385/1/crickreport1998.pdf.

Raines, J. C. (ed.) (2019) *Evidence-Based Practice in School Mental Health: Addressing DSM-5 Disorders in Schools*, 2nd edn. New York: Oxford University Press.

Rebughini, P. (2014) Subject, subjectivity, subjectivation. *Sociopedia.isa*. Available at: https://www.researchgate.net/publication/264466714_Subject_ subjectivity_subjectivation.

Riehm, K. E., Feder, K. A., Tormohlen, K. N., Crum, R. M., Young, A. S., Green, K. M., Pacek, L. R., La Flair, L. N. and Mojtabai, R. (2019) Associations between time spent using social media and internalizing and externalizing problems among US youth. *JAMA Psychiatry*, 76(12): 1266–1273. DOI: 10.1001/ jamapsychiatry.2019.2325

Riley, P. (2011) *Attachment Theory and the Teacher–Student Relationship: A Practical Guide for Teachers, Teacher Educators and School Leaders*. Abingdon and New York: Routledge.

Ringrose, J. (2008) 'Just be friends': exposing the limits of educational bully discourses for understanding teen girls' heterosexualized friendships and conflicts. *British Journal of Sociology of Education*, 29(5): 509-522. DOI: 10.1080/01425690802263668

Roberts, J. (2018) Restorative justice 'undermining teachers'. *TES* (7 June). Available at: https://www.tes.com/news/restorative-justice-undermining-teachers.

Robinson, M. (2013) *Trivium 21c: Preparing Young People for the Future with Lessons from the Past*. Carmarthen: Independent Thinking Press.

Robinson, M. (2014) Character education is a waste of time. *Trivium 21c* (4 November). Available at: https://trivium21c.com/2014/11/04/character-education-is-a-waste-of-time/.

Robinson, M. (2019) *Curriculum: Athena versus the Machine*. Carmarthen: Crown House Publishing.

Rogers, B. (2011) *You Know the Fair Rule: Strategies for Positive and Effective Behaviour Management and Discipline in Schools*, 3rd edn. Camberwell, VIC: ACER Press.

Rose, N. (2019) Attachment theory: what do teachers need to know? *researchED* [blog] (28 February). Available at: https://researchED.org.uk/attachment-theory-what-do-teachers-need-to-know/.

Rosenshine, B. (2012) Principles of instruction: research-based strategies that all teachers should know. *American Educator*, 36(1): 12-19, 39. Available at: https://www.aft.org/sites/default/files/periodicals/Rosenshine.pdf.

Rosenthal, R. and Jacobson, L. (1968). *Pygmalion in the Classroom: Teacher Expectation and Pupils' Intellectual Development*. New York: Holt, Rinehart and Winston.

Rousseau, J. J. (1979 [1762]) *Emile: Or on Education*, tr. A. Bloom. New York: Basic Books.

Rutter, M. (2015) Adolescence: biology, epidemiology, and process considerations. In G. Oettingen and P. Gollwitzer (eds), *Self-Regulation in Adolescence* (The Jacobs Foundation Series on Adolescence). Cambridge: Cambridge University Press, pp. 123-146.

Sanderse, W. (2019) Does neo-Aristotelian character education maintain the educational status quo? Lessons from the 19th-century *Bildung* tradition. *Ethics and Education*, 14(4): 399-414. DOI: 10.1080/17449642.2019.1660456

Schraer, R. (2019a) Knife crime: Are school exclusions to blame? *BBC News*. (8 March). Available at: https://www.bbc.co.uk/news/uk-47485867.

Schraer, R. (2019b) Is young people's mental health getting worse? *BBC News* (11 February). Available at: https://www.bbc.co.uk/news/health-47133338.

Sealy, C. (2019) Curriculum as boxset. Presentation given at CurriculumEd2019, Litchfield Cathedral School (1 June). Available at: https://www.lichfieldcathedralschool.com/conference-speakers/2098903.html.

Seymour, K. E., Mostofsky, S. H. and Rosch, K. S. (2016) Cognitive load differentially impacts response control in girls and boys with ADHD. *Journal of Abnormal Child Psychology*, 44(1): 141-154. DOI: 10.1007/s10802-015-9976-z

Short, R., Case, G. and McKenzie, K. (2018) The long-term impact of a whole school approach of restorative practice: the views of secondary school teachers. *Pastoral Care in Education*, 36(4): 313-324. DOI: 10.1080/02643944.2018.1528625

Siljander, P., Kivelä, A. and Sutinen, A. (2012) *Theories of* Bildung *and Growth: Connections and Controversies Between Continental Educational Thinking and American Pragmatism*. Rotterdam: Sense Publishers.

Smith, M. K. (2019) What is praxis? *The Encyclopaedia of Informal Education* (19 October). Available at: http://infed.org/mobi/what-is-praxis/.

Smith, N. (2019) *Back to School? Breaking the Link Between School Exclusions and Knife Crime*. London: All-Party Parliamentary Group on Knife Crime. Available at: http://www.preventknifecrime.co.uk/wp-content/uploads/2019/10/APPG-on-Knife-Crime-Back-to-School-exclusions-report-FINAL.pdf.

Sobel, D. (2019) *Leading on Pastoral Care: A Guide to Improving Outcomes for Every Student* [Kindle edn]. London: Bloomsbury.

Song, S. Y. and Swearer, S. M. (2016) The cart before the horse: the challenge and promise of restorative justice consultation in schools. *Journal of Educational and Psychological Consultation*, 26(4): 313–324. DOI: 10.1080/10474412.2016.1246972

Speck, D. (2019) Exclusive: Restorative behaviour policies 'leading to teacher-blaming'. *TES* (5 February). Available at: https://www.tes.com/news/exclusive-restorative-behaviour-policies-leading-teacher-blaming.

Staufenberg, J. (2019) DfE faces legal action over 'confusing' guidance on isolation booths. *Schools Week* (3 April). Available at: https://schoolsweek.co.uk/dfe-faces-legal-action-over-confusing-guidance-on-isolation-booths.

Steer, A. (2009) *Learning Behaviour: Lessons Learned. A Review of Behaviour Standards and Practices in Our Schools* [Steer Report]. Ref: DCSF-00453-2009. Annesley: Department for Children, Schools and Families. Available at: http://www.educationengland.org.uk/documents/pdfs/2009-steer-report-lessons-learned.pdf.

Sweller, J., Ayres, P. and Kalyuga, S. (2011) *Cognitive Load Theory*. New York: Springer.

Taylor, C. (2011) Getting the simple things right: Charlie Taylor's behaviour checklists. Available at: https://assets.publishing.service.gov.uk/government/uploads/system/uploads/attachment_data/file/571640/Getting_the_simple_things_right_Charlie_Taylor_s_behaviour_checklists.pdf.

Titcombe, R. (2019) Quality education needs thinking schools, not behaviour tsars or hero innovators. *Roger Titcombe's Learning Matters* [blog] (16 September). Available at: https://rogertitcombelearningmatters.wordpress.com/2019/09/16/quality-education-needs-thinking-schools-not-behaviour-tzars-or-hero-innovators/.

Trotman, D. (2016) Towards a spiritual pedagogy of pastoral welfare and care. *Pastoral Care in Education*, 34(3): 122–132. DOI: 10.1080/02643944.2016.1204350

Trotman, D. (2019) Creativity as a pastoral concern. *Pastoral Care in Education*, 37(1): 73–80. DOI: 10.1080/02643944.2019.1569844

Vaandering, D. (2014) Implementing restorative justice practice in schools: what pedagogy reveals. *Journal of Peace Education*, 11(1): 64–80. DOI: 10.1080/17400201.2013.794335

Walker, M., Sims, D. and Kettlewell, K. (2017) *Leading Character Education in Schools: Case Study Report*. Slough: NFER. Available at: https://www.nfer.ac.uk/media/2067/pace02.pdf.

Weale, S. (2019a) Teaching union calls zero-tolerance school policies 'inhumane'. *The Guardian* (17 April). Available at: https://www.theguardian.com/education/2019/apr/17/teaching-union-calls-zero-tolerance-school-policies-inhumane.

Weale, S. (2019b) Reform school exclusions to tackle knife crime, MPs urge. *The Guardian* (25 October). Available at: https://www.theguardian.com/uk-news/2019/oct/25/reform-school-exclusions-to-tackle-knife-mps-urge.

Weale, S. (2020a) One in four young people with mental health referral 'rejected'. *The Guardian* (10 January). Available at: https://www.theguardian.com/society/2020/jan/10/one-in-four-children-with-mental-health-referral-rejected-nhs.

Weale, S. (2020b) Schools 'converting toilet blocks into isolation booths'. *The Guardian* (17 January). Available at: https://www.theguardian.com/education/2020/jan/17/schools-converting-toilet-blocks-into-isolation-booths.

Whieldon, F. (2019) Harford: Ofsted has 'real issues' inspecting behaviour. *Schools Week* (1 June). Available at: https://schoolsweek.co.uk/harford-ofsted-has-real-issues-inspecting-behaviour/.

Whittaker, F. (2019) 'No exclusions from London schools' vows Lib Dem mayoral candidate. *Schools Week* (17 September). Available at: https://schoolsweek.co.uk/no-exclusions-from-london-schools-vows-lib-dem-mayoral-candidate.

Williams, J. (2018) *'It Just Grinds You Down': Persistent Disruptive Behaviour in Schools and What Can Be Done About It*. London: Policy Exchange. Available at: https://policyexchange.org.uk/wp-content/uploads/2019/01/It-Just-Grinds-You-Down-Joanna-Williams-Policy-Exchange-December-2018.pdf.

Winslade, J. and Williams, M. (2012) *Safe and Peaceful Schools: Addressing Conflict and Eliminating Violence*. Thousand Oaks, CA: Corwin Press.

Young, T. (2014) Why schools can't teach character. *The Spectator* (8 November). Available at: https://www.spectator.co.uk/2014/11/toby-young-status-anxiety-2/.